Life-Changing Devotionals

The Love and Mercy of God as Seen in Jonah, Job, and Joseph

TS Taylor

All for the Glory of God

Copyright © 2021

All rights reserved.

ISBN: 9798510754988

Cover Photograph: Image by kolibri5 from Pixabay

Scripture taken from the New King James Version®. Copyright © 1982 by Thomas Nelson. Used by permission. All rights reserved.

Printed in the United States of America

Contents

Introduction i
Section I – Jonah 1
Section II – Job 20
    In God's Throne Room 21
    Job and His Friends 31
    God Shows Up 77
Section III – The Life of Joseph 109
Concluding Thoughts 153

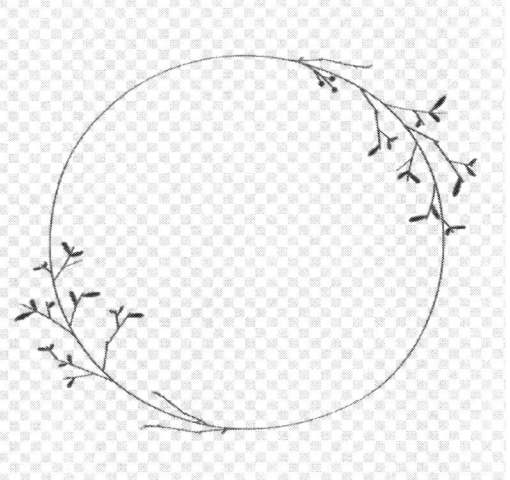

*"I cried out to the L*ORD *because of my affliction, and He answered me."*
(Jonah 2:2)

Introduction

You might find this to be a different style of devotional. Together we will walk through some stories from the Bible. Hopefully you will find some life-changing thoughts and questions along the way.

Tom S Taylor

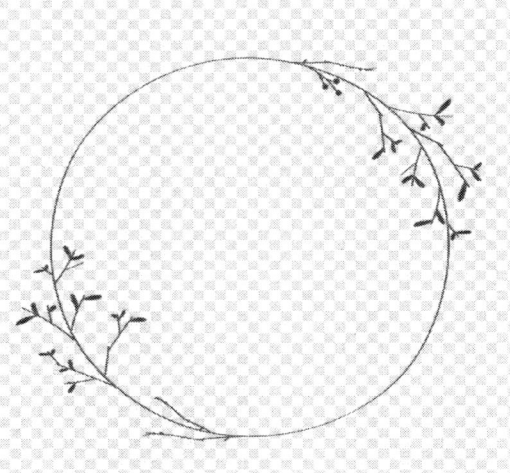

I. Jonah

In this study of Jonah, you will find a man who is given a task by God. He does not want to do it, so he tries to run away from the task and from God Himself.

Let's see how that turns out.

Jonah 1:1-3 – Can We Run Away?

¹ Now the word of the L<small>ORD</small> came to Jonah the son of Amittai, saying, ² "Arise, go to Nineveh, that great city, and cry out against it; for their wickedness has come up before Me." ³ But Jonah arose to flee to Tarshish from the presence of the L<small>ORD</small>. He went down to Joppa, and found a ship going to Tarshish; so he paid the fare, and went down into it, to go with them to Tarshish from the presence of the L<small>ORD</small>.

We can learn a lot about Jonah, and ourselves, from the first three verses of the book of Jonah. We learn that Jonah has the gift of preaching because God calls him to go to the great city of Nineveh and preach against it. We also see that God gives Jonah a difficult task: he is to preach against the wickedness in the city of Nineveh.

In verse 3, we see a word that we often find in the Scriptures: "but." Jonah does not want to do the task God has given him, so he tries to run away from the LORD.

How often do we do this when God gives us a task? For us, the task can sometimes be very simple, such as talking to our neighbor about what Jesus has done for us, doing an unexpected good deed for someone we really don't like, or helping out at church in a way we think is beneath us. There is no task too big, too small, or too unimportant for God to be involved with.

When we don't do the tasks that God has given us, we are like Jonah: we are trying to run away from the LORD. As we will see throughout the book of Jonah, this is a foolish endeavor. Trying to run away from the LORD never works. He is, after all, all-powerful and fully in charge of His creation. God's plan will not be thwarted by our disobedience. He always has ways to get us to do the tasks that He has for us.

When you find yourself thinking about running away from the LORD—stop! Turn around and don't do it! You might end up in the belly of a fish for three days.

Do you really think you can run away from the LORD?

Notes:

Jonah 1:4-6 – Jonah Is Asleep

⁴ But the LORD *sent out a great wind on the sea, and there was a mighty tempest on the sea, so that the ship was about to be broken up.*

⁵ Then the mariners were afraid; and every man cried out to his god, and threw the cargo that was in the ship into the sea, to lighten the load. But Jonah had gone down into the lowest parts of the ship, had lain down, and was fast asleep.

⁶ So the captain came to him, and said to him, "What do you mean, sleeper? Arise, call on your God; perhaps your God will consider us, so that we may not perish."

Jonah is trying to run away from the task God has given him. He is on a ship bound for Tarshish—a place at the farthest reaches of the known world. However, the LORD sends a great wind on the sea to create a violent storm. The storm is so great that the ship is on the verge of breaking apart and even the seasoned sailors are terrified. They are calling out to their pagan, idol gods. They are taking things into their own hands by throwing cargo into the sea to lighten the ship.

This is a wonderful description of us and the world today. The world is taking problems into its own hands rather than seeking the LORD and His justice and mercy. The world has removed the LORD from the classrooms, the universities, the courtrooms, the public square and our businesses. A great storm is brewing; where are the Christians?

We find Jonah asleep below deck. How can Jonah possibly be asleep with this storm going on? The reason is that Jonah has been consumed and exhausted by the task of running away from the LORD: finding the ship going to Tarshish, paying the fare, and making sure he brought enough money and clothes. He has been focused on the many mundane tasks he has prioritized for himself, rather than the one big task that the LORD has given him.

Like Jonah, we can often be so worn out and preoccupied with the activities of daily life and our own priorities that when the storms of life come, we are asleep. Like Jonah, we try to do too much by ourselves and for ourselves without the LORD's help or guidance.

The only way that you can stay awake is to carve out time to spend with the LORD even when things are crazy and busy. This quiet time of preparation will brace you for the chaos and provide guidance when the storm breaks. "But seek first the kingdom of God and His righteousness, and all these things shall be added to you" (Matthew 6:33).

Do you want your Captain to find you asleep when there is such a great task at hand?

Notes:

Jonah 1:11-12 – What Should We Do?

¹¹ Then they said to him, "What shall we do to you that the sea may be calm for us?"—for the sea was growing more tempestuous.

¹² And he said to them, "Pick me up and throw me into the sea; then the sea will become calm for you. For I know that this great tempest is because of me."

The sailors have cast lots to try to determine who is responsible for this great storm. The lot falls on Jonah. They ask him who he is, what he is doing, and what country and people he is from. Jonah declares that he is a Hebrew and he worships "the LORD, the God of heaven, who made the sea and the dry land."

This terrifies the sailors. What does this mean? The storm continues to get more tempestuous. Their world is falling apart around them. They have someone in their midst who has unmistakably declared his allegiance to the Creator of the world. So they ask Jonah, "What shall we do?"

This is the role we need to fill in our world today. We need to acknowledge the storm around us. We need to acknowledge that we cannot fix these problems alone. We need to help others see that they also cannot fix these problems alone. We need to declare that we worship the LORD, the God of heaven, who made the seas and the land. He is the one who can offer forgiveness for our sins. He can change the hearts of those who have lost their way. He is the one who can shape new lives.

When we stand up as people of the Light in a dark world, the world will take notice. The world might then ask you, "What shall we do?" Will you be ready to answer this question? It will not be easy to stand up and declare that God is the only One who can fix the storms of the heart. We cannot fix these storms without Him.

Jonah responds with an act of self-sacrifice. He says that he must be thrown into the sea to stop the storm. Did Jonah know what would happen next? Did the LORD tell him of the next step in His plan? No! However, Jonah knew what his current task was. He knew that he messed up and that he needed to trust the LORD with the next step. This was not easy for Jonah, but he did it.

Would you volunteer to be thrown overboard into the stormy sea?

Notes:

Jonah 1:13-17 – The LORD Provided

¹³ Nevertheless the men rowed hard to return to land, but they could not, for the sea continued to grow more tempestuous against them. ¹⁴ Therefore they cried out to the LORD and said, "We pray, O LORD, please do not let us perish for this man's life, and do not charge us with innocent blood; for You, O LORD, have done as it pleased You." ¹⁵ So they picked up Jonah and threw him into the sea, and the sea ceased from its raging. ¹⁶ Then the men feared the LORD exceedingly, and offered a sacrifice to the LORD and took vows.

¹⁷ Now the LORD had prepared a great fish to swallow Jonah. And Jonah was in the belly of the fish three days and three nights.

After throwing Jonah into the sea, the sailors offer a sacrifice to the one true God, Yahweh, and make vows to Him. We see that Jonah proclaiming his faith to the one true God has had a big impact on the sailors.

Verse 17 starts with a hopeful phrase: "now the LORD." When we hear this phrase, we might expect to hear a great story about angel armies and heavenly chariots coming to rescue Jonah. Or perhaps a story like the parting of the Red Sea. Maybe Jonah will grab onto a piece of floating driftwood in the raging sea and then dolphins will carry him to shore.

After we read "now the LORD had prepared," we do not expect to read "a huge fish to swallow Jonah." Notice that the language here is very intentional. The LORD picked this unusual method of saving Jonah before the foundation of the earth. So it is with us; the LORD has already picked out a method to save you from disaster. It may be a very conventional and convenient method for you, or it may be as scary as being swallowed by a big fish. But know this: God will use the right method at the right time.

It must have been incredibly scary for Jonah to stare into the gaping mouth of the great fish as he was being swallowed. Inside the belly of the fish, it was probably dark, cold, and slimy. This is not the kind of place we think of to spend quiet time with the LORD, much less a three-day and three-night journey. But in the quiet of the fish's belly, Jonah does not have anything to do except be still and recognize that God is in charge, not Jonah. This is what the LORD requires of Jonah: to spend time focusing on who God is and who Jonah is.

This is one of the most important exercises we can do: focus on who God is and who we are. We will not know who we are until we really understand who God is.

For you to grab ahold of this, do you need to be in the belly of the fish for three days?

Notes:

Jonah 2:2,9 – He Answered Me

"I cried out to the LORD because of my affliction, and He answered me."
(Jonah 2:2)

"Salvation is of the LORD."
(Jonah 2:9)

From inside the belly of the fish, Jonah prays to the LORD. His prayer begins, "I cried out to the LORD... And He answered me." I have often wondered what Jonah's first prayers were like. I suspect they started with questions like: Why? How long will I be here? Did I really deserve this? Have You abandoned me? Can You hear my pitiful prayers? Will I get another chance?

We see that Jonah called out to God in prayer and Jonah knew God answered him by sending a big fish to swallow him. How do we know that God answers our prayers? Knowing that God answers our prayers means we must listen to God. Prayer is two-way communication: we spend a lot of time talking to God, telling Him what we need, but we should also spend a lot of time listening to God. "Listening to God" can be quiet meditation, reading His Word, or even studying the lives of some of the saints.

I believe that Jonah gets answers to many of his questions. Jonah recognizes he is in the fish's belly because he needs to meditate more on the character of God and what He is going to do in the world. He understands he will be inside the fish until he is ready to go do the task God had given him to do. He sees that God did not abandon him. He realizes that God always hears his prayers.

Jonah discovers that from the depths of the grave, God can hear his prayer. In the storms of life, God can rescue him. When he is brought so low, to the moorings of the mountains, God can still raise him up. When his own strength is ebbing away, he knows that God's grace will be sufficient for him.

He ends his prayer with "Salvation is of the LORD." Jonah has come to a much deeper understanding of who God is and how much He loves him. Now Jonah is ready to go do the task God had given him.

Are you ready to go do your task?

Notes:

Jonah 2:10, 3:5 – The Ninevites Believed God

¹⁰ So the Lord spoke to the fish, and it vomited Jonah onto dry land.

⁵ So the people of Nineveh believed God, proclaimed a fast, and put on sackcloth, from the greatest to the least of them.

Chapter 2 of Jonah ends with a rather dramatic start for a ministry: "So the Lord spoke to the fish, and it vomited Jonah onto dry land." What a way to start a new ministry—by being vomited onto the shore!

Next, we read that the word of the Lord came to Jonah a second time, showing us that God is indeed a God of second chances. He allows us to fail, get picked up, and try again. God will continually be holding His mighty right hand out to us that we might walk with Him, even after we have stumbled. God's plans will not be thwarted. He will continue to use His people to do good works.

Jonah goes into the city of Nineveh. It is so large it requires three days to visit the whole city. Jonah begins proclaiming his message of woe: "Yet forty days, and Nineveh shall be overthrown."

Chapter 3, verse 5 gives us an interesting twist in the story. It reads, "the people of Nineveh believed God." Notice it does not say that the Ninevites heard Jonah's message, understood Jonah's message, and believed Jonah.

I'm sure at this point Jonah is really proud of himself for doing the task God had given him. Perhaps he sees himself as overcoming great adversity and is feeling a great deal of self-pride. But we read that all the hard work has been done by the LORD. He is the one who was preparing the hearts of the Ninevites before Jonah arrived, and He is the one who changed the Ninevites' hearts. Jonah just had to do the task God had given him to do.

It is the same with us. God gives us tasks to perform. With each of these tasks, God does the hard work beforehand. We cannot change anyone's heart with our logic, our proclamations, or even our love. Only the Holy Spirit changes hearts. He will be preparing people's hearts for the message. We just need to go and do the task.

Are you ready to go and see whose heart God has prepared?

Notes:

Jonah 4:1-4 – Jonah Is Angry

¹ But it displeased Jonah exceedingly, and he became angry. ² So he prayed to the LORD, and said, "Ah, LORD, was not this what I said when I was still in my country? Therefore I fled previously to Tarshish; for I know that You are a gracious and merciful God, slow to anger and abundant in lovingkindness, One who relents from doing harm. ³ Therefore now, O LORD, please take my life from me, for it is better for me to die than to live!"

⁴ Then the LORD said, "Is it right for you to be angry?"

Chapter 4 also has a dramatic twist: Jonah is angry because God is merciful. Jonah calls out to God, acknowledging that He is gracious and merciful, slow to anger, and abundant in lovingkindness. Why then should Jonah be angry?

Jonah is angry because God has blessed his enemies. When we read that Jesus tells us to pray for our enemies, we often misunderstand what He is saying. We are to pray that our enemies will turn to Christ, cease from their evil, repent, and turn from their wickedness. This is exactly what has happened with the city of Nineveh. But Jonah is angry about it. He is angry because the Ninevites were his enemies. He really wanted God to destroy them, but God did not destroy them - He caused them to repent.

Unfortunately, we are a lot like this today. We often pray half-heartedly for our enemies. Do you pray earnestly that your enemies will repent and turn from their wickedness? We forget that God is the one who changes hearts. Through the story of Jonah, God is telling us to continue praying earnestly for our enemies, that the Holy Spirit would work in their hearts. We are to go about doing the tasks that God has given us: to speak to people about the truth of the gospel and to love them. God will do the rest.

When He does a great work, will we have any right to be angry?

Notes:

Jonah 4:9-11 – Jonah's Priorities

⁹ Then God said to Jonah, "Is it right for you to be angry about the plant?"

And he said. "It is right for me to be angry, even to death!"

*¹⁰ But the L*ORD *said, "You have had pity on the plant for which you have not labored, nor made it grow, which came up in a night and perished in a night. ¹¹ And should I not pity Nineveh, that great city, in which are more than one hundred and twenty thousand persons who cannot discern between their right hand and their left—and much livestock?"*

Chapter 4 of Jonah ends with an interesting story about a vine that God grows to bless Jonah with cool shade. God then takes the vine away and Jonah gets angry about it. God is using this situation to help Jonah understand his priorities. Jonah is more concerned about his physical comfort than he is about the spiritual state of the people of Nineveh.

In verse 9, God asks Jonah, "Is it right for you to be angry about the plant?" God goes on to tell Jonah that Jonah did not make the vine grow, nor did he tend to it or water it. It came up by the providential will of God. Yet, Jonah is more concerned about the vine than he is about the people of Nineveh.

God ends the book of Jonah with a question: "And should I not pity Nineveh, that great city?" I am fascinated that this book of the Bible ends with a question. This is very rare, as most books of the Bible end with a proclamation or declaration. I believe the Holy Spirit is trying to draw us into this story even more by helping us understand what God is concerned about.

God is more concerned about the welfare of people's spiritual state than he is about their physical comfort. So it should be with us. Yes, we should be concerned about people's physical state (Are they naked, hungry, or lonely? If so, reach out to them), but we should be more concerned about their eternal state. This is indeed a difficult task for us to understand in our daily lives. God wants us to understand what He is most concerned about.

Are you concerned about the spiritual state of your friends and neighbors?

Notes:

Matthew 12:38-41 – Jonah Points to Jesus

38 Then some of the scribes and Pharisees answered, saying, "Teacher, we want to see a sign from You."

39 But He answered and said to them, "An evil and adulterous generation seeks after a sign, and no sign will be given to it except the sign of the prophet Jonah. 40 For as Jonah was three days and three nights in the belly of the great fish, so will the Son of Man be three days and three nights in the heart of the earth. 41 The men of Nineveh will rise up in the judgment with this generation and condemn it, because they repented at the preaching of Jonah; and indeed a greater than Jonah is here.

There are two places in Matthew where Jesus refers to Jonah, this one in chapter 12 being the first.

The scribes and Pharisees want to see a sign from Jesus. A sign is a miracle that points from the miracle worker to God, which validates the worker's credibility. Jesus just healed a man with a withered hand. What more are the Pharisees looking for?

Jesus points the Pharisees back to Jonah as a sign. Jonah was given up for dead when he was tossed into the sea. If any of the sailors actually saw Jonah being swallowed by the great fish, they would have certainly declared him dead.

Three days later, Jonah appeared on the scene again, preaching repentance so that the people of Nineveh could come into a right relationship with God. They listened to Jonah's message and God worked in their hearts. They repented.

Not so for the Pharisees in Matthew's Gospel. The Pharisees still refuse to believe in Jesus despite seeing many signs that pointed to Him as the Messiah. Jesus tells them that Jonah's story was a foreshadowing of the death and resurrection of Jesus the Messiah. Like Jonah being in the belly of the great fish for three days, Jesus will be in the belly of the earth for three days. If the Pharisees do not repent once they see this final, majestic sign from Jesus Himself, they will be condemned by the example of the people of Nineveh, who were smart enough to listen to the word of God.

Don't you be condemned by the example of the people of Nineveh on the last day.

If you have not already, will you accept Jesus as your personal Savior?

Notes:

II. Job

Much of the Old Testament is a study of God's character. You will get to see several sides of God's character in the story of Job.

First, as seen from God's throne room, then as envisioned by Job and his friends, and finally by God Himself.

In God's Throne Room

This is a unique glimpse of God in His throne room with the angels in attendance. Satan, a fallen angel, is also in attendance. He has come from walking back and forth on the earth. Satan is looking for a way to defeat God or at least tarnish His glory. God's ultimate objective is to show that He is omnipotent. He is in charge and will bring about His good, even when Satan means it for evil.

Job 1:1 – A Man of Integrity

¹ There was a man in the land of Uz, whose name was Job; and that man was blameless and upright, and one who feared God and shunned evil.

The book of Job starts with a very interesting introduction. Job is introduced as a man who is blameless and upright. He fears God and shuns evil.

Many people struggle with the description of "blameless" in Job 1:1. We all know that Job is not blameless in the sense of being sinless. The Scriptures teach that all people are sinners, even those whose hearts are fully turned toward God.

The word "blameless" in this verse means "integrity." We think of a person of integrity as being honest, having strong moral principles, and being morally upright. This is a very good description of Job. Job always tries to do the right things in life. He fears God. This motivates him to stay on the straight and narrow and keep his heart and life turned toward God in all circumstances.

Job is also described as upright. In Job's day, "upright" meant not to be twisted or bent. In today's language, we would say that his moral compass was pointed due north.

Another aspect of Job's character is that he shuns evil. This is a wonderful description of somebody who is morally upright. Not only does he do the right thing, but he actively avoids doing the wrong thing.

We will see later in Job's character description that he was known to give to those in need, take care of weary travelers, and provide for others. He was a respected man in his city. While Job was a wealthy man, he used his wealth for the good of others.

If we saw somebody like Job today, we would want to be like him. We would try to emulate him with our good works. Job exemplifies what it means to be good, do the right thing, and be a person of integrity.

After you die, will someone write on your tombstone "a person of integrity"?

Notes:

Job 1:6-7 – Satan Prowls Like a Lion

6 Now there was a day when the sons of God came to present themselves before the LORD, and Satan also came among them. 7 And the LORD said to Satan, "From where do you come?"

So Satan answered the LORD and said, "From going to and fro on the earth, and from walking back and forth on it."

The book of Job continues with a dramatic scene of the Heavenly Court. The LORD Almighty is on His throne and the angels have come to present themselves before Him. Satan, a fallen angel, also comes before the LORD. The LORD asks Satan where he has come from. Satan replies, "From going to and fro on the earth, and from walking back and forth on it."

We see from this reply that Satan has his dominion on the earth. He is prowling to cause evil. The question is, what is he looking for? We see the answer to this question in 1 Peter 5:8-9:

"Be sober, be vigilant; because your adversary the devil walks about like a roaring lion, seeking whom he may devour. Resist him, steadfast in the faith, knowing that the same sufferings are experienced by your brotherhood in the world."

Satan is looking for someone to devour. Satan is trying to tarnish the glory of God Almighty. Satan knows he has lost the war, but he is still trying to win a few minor battles. Satan hates the LORD Almighty and all that is good. He cannot stand the fact he is not seated on the throne of all that is. Satan's tactic is to try to make God's creatures turn against their Creator. In this case, Satan is trying to devour you and me. He will do this through lies, deceit, and jealousy, just to name a few of his tricks.

Peter tells us to resist and remain steadfast in the faith. Being steadfast in the faith means that we are not standing alone, but under the protection of Jesus, the Lamb of God who was slain for our sins. Satan is too powerful for us to overcome on our own. We need the protection of the LORD Almighty.

When Satan comes into your world, will you be ready to resist him?

Notes:

Job 1:9-12 – A Hedge of Protection

⁹ So Satan answered the Lord and said, "Does Job fear God for nothing? ¹⁰ Have You not made a hedge around him, around his household, and around all that he has on every side? You have blessed the work of his hands, and his possessions have increased in the land. ¹¹ But now, stretch out Your hand and touch all that he has, and he will surely curse You to Your face!" ¹² And the Lord said to Satan, "Behold, all that he has is in your power; only do not lay a hand on his person."

This section of the book of Job describes one of the most powerful defenses we have against the Evil One. Satan is in the Heavenly Court trying to tarnish the glory of the Lord Almighty. Satan wants to use Job to accomplish this by getting Job to curse God to His face.

The Lord reminds Satan that Job is a man who is blameless and upright. Satan's response is that Job is only this way because the Lord has put a hedge of protection around him, his household, and all he has.

This hedge of protection is one of the most important concepts in Scripture concerning our defense against the Evil One. The Evil One is far too strong for us to resist on our own. We need the protection of the Lord Almighty.

This part of Job paints a picture of a hedge. Imagine a thick, tall, green hedge around your property and family. This hedge is so thick and tall that no one can walk through it. It is a sure defense against a roaring lion. However, there is one way through the thick hedge: the gate. We are in control of the gate. We can open the gate. Satan will tempt us from the other side of the hedge to get us to open the gate. He will use any trick he can, such as offering many riches or poking at our pride. If we open the gate, he can come in.

The hedge is there for your protection. Continually pray that God would build this hedge around you and your household. Pray that He weaves more leaves and branches in the hedge to make it thicker and stronger. Pray that you will lock the gate so the Evil One cannot enter.

Will you pray for a hedge of protection around your household today?

Notes:

Job 1:20-22 – Job Worships

[20] *Then Job arose, tore his robe, and shaved his head; and he fell to the ground and worshiped.* [21] *And he said:*

*"Naked I came from my mother's womb,
And naked shall I return there.
The LORD gave, and the LORD has taken away;
Blessed be the name of the LORD."*

[22] *In all this Job did not sin nor charge God with wrong.*

After God agrees to remove the hedge of protection around Job's household, Satan wreaks havoc on Job's life. Job's family is killed and all his livestock and valuable possessions are taken away. This is a horrible time in Job's life.

What is amazing about Job's character is that when he hears this news, he tears his robe, shaves his head in mourning, and then he falls to the ground and... worships God!

You would think we would find Job yelling at God, being angry at God, ignoring God, or just generally being furious. However, we read that Job falls to the ground and worships.

This is really amazing! In response to great personal calamity, Job worships the LORD. We see from the text that Job knows God is his creator. Job knows that everything he has is from the LORD God Almighty. Job knows that God is in charge. In all things, good or bad, Job knows that God is to be praised and worshiped. Job knows that even when he walks in the valley of the shadow of death, God is still there with him. What Job is really worshipping about God is the fact that God is with him, even in this time of great calamity.

In times of great calamity, it is difficult for us to remember that God is with us and that He is in charge. We have trouble seeing how horrible events can be connected to a loving and merciful God. However, we must remember our hope comes from knowing that God is with us.

When calamity strikes, will you be able to fall down and worship the LORD?

Notes:

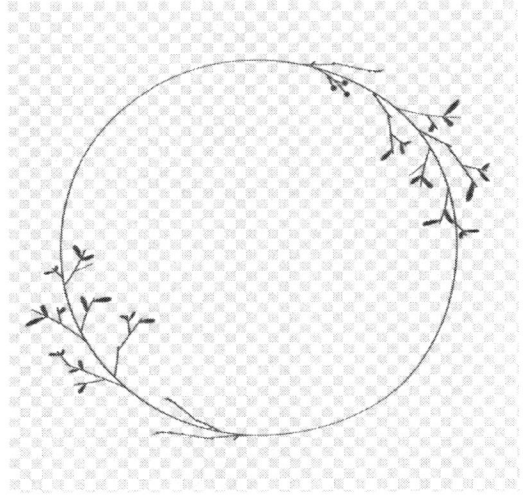

Job and His Friends

Several of Job's friends show up to comfort him. As you will see, they are not very good comforters. However, you will get a glimpse of God's character, the nature of evil and what it means to live a life of integrity.

Job 2:11-13 – Job's Friends Show Up

¹³ So they sat down with him on the ground seven days and seven nights, and no one spoke a word to him, for they saw that his grief was very great.

After killing all of Job's sons and daughters and taking away all his wealth and possessions, Satan inflicts a horrible skin disease upon Job. However, Job still does not give up on God, nor does he curse God.

Three of Job's friends come to visit him and comfort him. They heard about Job's trouble and set out from their homes to sympathize with him. The most significant part of their visit is that they sit on the ground with Job for seven days and seven nights without saying a word to him.

The hardest part of comforting a grieving person is knowing what to say. Often we do nothing because we are paralyzed by our own fear. We know that we should reach out to the grieving person, but how do we comfort him or her? We feel very awkward and uncomfortable in this situation. For example, many people don't like visiting sick and suffering friends who are in the hospital. We don't like seeing people in great pain and grief. We just don't want to be there.

Often the most loving thing you can do is just show up. You don't need to have a plan or a speech to deliver. You don't need to know why bad things happen in the world. In fact, you don't need to say anything at all. You just need to show up and be there to listen to the grieving person.

As we will see later in the book of Job, Job's friends are not very good comforters. But at least they got the first part right: they showed up and offered their time to be there for Job. In their case, they were with him for a week before they said anything. Often the best thing you can do is just show up and be there as a friend.

The next time a friend of yours is in need of comfort, would you just show up and be there?

Notes:

Job 3:11-12 – Job's First Lament: "Why?"

11 "Why did I not die at birth?
Why did I not perish when I came from the womb?
12 Why did the knees receive me?
Or why the breasts, that I should nurse?"

Job chapter 3 begins with Job's first lament. A lament is a passionate expression of grief or sorrow – two emotions that Job is obviously feeling. In this lament, Job asks the question "why?" many times. This is usually the first kind of question we ask when pain and grief come our way. We are always pleased when God blesses us beyond what we deserve. We thank him because we have come to expect these blessings. However, when bad things come into our lives, we let God know of our displeasure. Why are these bad things happening to me? How am I going to deal with this? Where is God in this dilemma? When bad things happen, we often lose our way.

It is good to see that Job, a man who was upright and blameless, also struggled with the same questions. Notice that even in Job's pain and grief, he continues to worship God. He is comfortable enough in his relationship with God that he can ask God "why" questions. He can get angry at God for the things that have happened to him. He can struggle with these issues and try to understand what God is teaching him. But in all these things, Job never sins or curses God.

This is such a difficult time for Job that he wishes he was never born. We have all felt like this at one point or another. But even during difficult times, we need to remember that God is in charge, He loves us, and all things are working for His glory. We may find out why bad things happen in our lives during our time on earth, but we may not understand why until we get to heaven.

Are you comfortable enough in your relationship with God to ask the question "why?" and not get a clear answer right away? If not, what can you do to help get yourself in that place?

Notes:

Job 4:8 – Reap What You Sow

*"Even as I have seen,
Those who plow iniquity
And sow trouble reap the same."
(Job 4:8)*

*Do not be deceived, God is not mocked; for whatever a man sows, that he will also reap. For he who sows to his flesh will of the flesh reap corruption, but he who sows to the Spirit will of the Spirit reap everlasting life.
(Galatians 6:7-8)*

In chapter 4, Eliphaz, the eldest of the three comforters, begins his response to Job's lament. Job's friends often respond to his lamenting by telling him he deserves the punishment that God is giving him. This is an important age-old question: do we get punished by God because we did something to deserve it?

We see from Eliphaz's response that he definitely believes God is punishing Job because of something Job has done. There is wisdom in the idea that "we reap what we sow." We see it also in Paul's letter to the Galatians.

We've seen this in our own lives. When we do something really stupid or horrible, these things often come back to haunt us. We sometimes ruin really good things in our lives by committing great and grievous sins. In these cases, it is true that we reap what we sow.

But there are other times in life when bad things come our way for reasons that we do not know or understand. God may be working a great plan in which our suffering is an important part, but the details of the plan are often unknown to us. This can be frustrating.

But we know that God loves us and He wants us to do good and loving acts. Even when bad things are happening to us, we are still called to love God and our neighbors. With some of the bad things that happen in our lives, we will be able to look back later and see how God used them for good. However, other bad things will just remain a mystery for now.

Even when bad things are happening in your life, can you go on and love God, yourself, and your neighbors?

Notes:

Job 9:4-10 – The LORD Almighty

⁴ "God is wise in heart and mighty in strength.
Who has hardened himself against Him and prospered?
⁵ He removes the mountains, and they do not know
When He overturns them in His anger;
⁶ He shakes the earth out of its place,
And its pillars tremble;
⁷ He commands the sun, and it does not rise;
He seals off the stars;
⁸ He alone spreads out the heavens,
And treads on the waves of the sea;
⁹ He made the Bear, Orion, and the Pleiades,
And the chambers of the south;
¹⁰ He does great things past finding out,
Yes, wonders without number."

In chapter 9, Job replies to the speech of Bildad, one of his comforters. In his reply, Job focuses on who God is. This is one of the most important lessons from the book of Job: to learn who God is and therefore learn who we are.

Job proclaims that God's wisdom is profound and vast. We cannot understand Him or stand against Him. His ways are beyond our ways. He perfectly balances power, wisdom, justice, and mercy. God's strength is unfathomable. He can remove mountains without us knowing. He can shake the earth and make it tremble. He can command the sun not to rise. He upholds all creation, and through Him all things are held together.

God's power stretches into the heavens and through the entire universe. He made the Bear, Orion, and the Pleiades. These are celestial wonders we can see in the northern hemisphere today. The Bear is the Big Dipper constellation, which is easily seen in the summer sky. Orion, also known as the Hunter, is a large constellation that dominates the winter sky. The Pleiades is an easily recognized star cluster just ahead of Orion. Even as Job saw these star patterns in the night sky in his time, we can still see them today.

It is comforting to recall the greatness of God – His wisdom, His strength, the scope of His created world, and His creativity. He continually shows us things that only He can do, such as forming constellations in the sky.

The next time you are out in God's creation, day or night, can you look around, see all that God has done, and recall His glory?

Notes:

Job 10:8-12 – The Potter and Clay

⁸ "'Your hands have made me and fashioned me,
An intricate unity;
Yet You would destroy me.
⁹ Remember, I pray, that You have made me like clay.
And will You turn me into dust again?
¹⁰ Did You not pour me out like milk,
And curdle me like cheese,
¹¹ Clothe me with skin and flesh,
And knit me together with bones and sinews?
¹² You have granted me life and favor,
And Your care has preserved my spirit.'"
(Job 10:8-12)

But now, O LORD,
You are our Father;
We are the clay, and You our potter;
And all we are the work of Your hand.
(Isaiah 64:8)

In chapter 10, we see Job struggling with this question: why are these calamities happening to me? He is speaking to God, not his comforters. In this section, Job acknowledges that God is the potter and he is the clay. God is the one who shapes us for the tasks and life He has planned for us. God has molded each of us to be His children. Job continues to wonder, as God's creature, why are these terrible things happening to me?

The illustration of the potter and the clay has several important aspects to it. The first is that God is in charge – He is the potter. He has full control over the clay. He created us because our chief end is to glorify God and enjoy Him forever.

Secondly, God created each of us individually and uniquely. Some of us are bowls, some of us are pitchers, and some of us are fine vases. God has created us uniquely for our own tasks, as we each have a special role to play in this world. God is laying out a huge banquet on earth for all His creation. Each of us will play a role at this banquet. Some roles will be high and mighty while other roles will be small, but all of them are important. Sometimes it takes a lifetime to understand what our role on earth is.

In times of great calamity, it is hard to understand why God has brought these difficult times upon us and how they contribute to our role on earth. Perhaps they are part of our maturing process.

Do you have a good understanding of what God has shaped you to do?

Notes:

Job 11:14-15 – Job, Jesus, and the Blind Man

[14] *"If iniquity were in your hand, and you put it far away,*
And would not let wickedness dwell in your tents;
[15] Then surely you could lift up your face without spot;
Yes, you could be steadfast, and not fear."
(Job 11:14-15)

[1] Now as Jesus passed by, He saw a man who was blind from birth. [2] And His disciples asked Him, saying, "Rabbi, who sinned, this man or his parents, that he was born blind?" [3] Jesus answered, "Neither this man nor his parents sinned, but that the works of God should be revealed in him."
(John 9:1-3)

Job's third comforter, Zophar, continues trying to convince Job that Job has some secret sin in his life. Zophar uses the expression "wickedness dwelling in your tents." Zophar believes God is punishing Job because of some secret, hidden sin. God does indeed punish sin and wickedness. Sometimes this happens directly in our lives on earth; however, some sins will not be punished until we go before the judgment seat of God. Zophar cannot see that God may be working some grand plan with Job and his calamity that has nothing to do with Job's personal sin.

The question of how God punishes sin also came up in Jesus' day. In chapter 9 of John, we find a man who was born blind. Was his blindness caused by his parents' sin or his own sin? Jesus says that it is neither – this man is blind so that the works of God might be displayed.

Jesus is the Light of the world. In His encounter with the blind man, Jesus used the man's blindness to show His power and glory. This answers some questions but leaves others unanswered. Will Jesus heal every blind person? No. Will the LORD cause every faithful believer to suffer like Job? No, probably not. Perhaps this is a more interesting question: If either Job or the blind man knew of their calamity before they were born, would they have chosen to accept their calamity so that the glory of God would be revealed, or would they have taken the easy way out and refused to accept?

If God gave you the choice to accept your present troubles for His glory, would you accept or pass?

Notes:

Job 11:7-9, 12:7-10 – The Hand of the LORD

⁷ "Can you search out the deep things of God?
Can you find out the limits of the Almighty?
⁸ They are higher than heaven—what can you do?
Deeper than Sheol—what can you know?
⁹ Their measure is longer than the earth
And broader than the sea."
(Job 11:7-9)

⁷ "But now ask the beasts, and they will teach you;
And the birds of the air, and they will tell you;
⁸ Or speak to the earth, and it will teach you;
And the fish of the sea will explain to you.
⁹ Who among all these does not know
That the hand of the LORD has done this,
¹⁰ In whose hand is the life of every living thing,
And the breath of all mankind?"
(Job 12:7-10)

Zophar reminds Job that Job cannot possibly know the deep things of God. They are higher than heaven and broader than the sea. Can any of us know the deep things of God? The breadth and depth of His wisdom? The place and majesty of His throne room? His role in sustaining the beasts, birds, fish, and you and me? Should we just give up on the task of knowing God and confine ourselves to ignorant lives?

Job tells Zophar that everything that happens in this world is done by the hand of the LORD. How can the deep things of God be so far beyond us, but at the same time God is intimately involved in the world around us?

Even the animals know of the intimate hand of the LORD. They know that God has their lives in His hands. He gives each of us our breath and our daily bread. He is so closely involved in the world around us that it should be obvious all of us. But we are often so busy going about our daily routines that we cannot see the blessings God brings our way.

Job is reminding both Zophar and ourselves to stop and look at the world around us. We need to count our blessings for just this day. When we stop to count our blessings, we begin to see that God is intimately involved in our world to bring Himself glory.

When you stop to look at all the blessings in your life, can you see the hand of the LORD?

Notes:

Job 12:23-25 – Great Nations

²³ "He makes nations great, and destroys them;
He enlarges nations, and guides them.
²⁴ He takes away the understanding of the chiefs of the people of the earth,
And makes them wander in a pathless wilderness.
²⁵ They grope in the dark without light,
And He makes them stagger like a drunken man."

Job is struggling to understand that God is the Lord of all. The LORD is sovereign over Job's suffering as well as all the problems of the nations.

Job reminds his friends that God makes nations great and He destroys them. No nation will last forever on this earth. Both the Egyptian pharaohs and the Roman emperors thought they would reign forever and ever. Where are they today?

It is hard for us to keep in mind that the nations of the world are put in place to work out a part of God's plan. What is even harder to grasp is that this same LORD is also LORD of our individual lives. He cares intimately about each of us. In fact, He cares more about us as individuals than He does for us as a collective nation.

God is weaving the great tapestry of life. The individual threads of this tapestry are individual people. The nations are the backdrop of the major scenes. God is using our lives to bring His kingdom to earth.

Why does Job bring up God's role amongst the nations amidst his great suffering? First, to remind us that we need to pray for our national and local leaders. Pray that they may listen to the wisdom of God and not grope in darkness. Secondly, we need to be engaged in our nation and our local community. We are to be the light of the world in places of darkness.

Ask God to give you wisdom and energy to stand up for the truth of God in a world darkened by man's folly. Love your neighbors so that they may see what it means to live a godly life. Pray for God to change the hearts of your nation's leaders as well as the hearts of your neighbors.

Can you pray for your nation's leaders and your neighbors right now?

Notes:

Job 13:4-7 – Worthless Physicians

⁴ "But you forgers of lies,
You are all worthless physicians.
⁵ Oh, that you would be silent,
And it would be your wisdom!
⁶ Now hear my reasoning,
And heed the pleadings of my lips.
⁷ Will you speak wickedly for God,
And talk deceitfully for Him?"

Job calls his friends "forgers of lies" and "worthless physicians" as they try to act as good comforters. In Job's day, as well as our own, physicians were respected in the community as people who brought great help and comfort. We expect physicians to bring healing and wisdom to situations at hand.

Job admonishes his friends to remain silent and wishes they would keep their wisdom to themselves. What is the reason for this? Job tells his friends that they speak wickedly for God by not understanding the full mind of God and His purposes on earth. They do not revere the majesty and complexity of God and His plans.

This is often true in our day as well. We feel compelled to try to cure someone's depression and hurt. We often bring worldly advice that conflicts with the word of God. We bring words that are empty of God's wisdom. Job is telling his friends that he does not need them to speak for God.

Job wants his friends to bring love and compassion. Perhaps they could bring a hot meal or send a handwritten note expressing their love. Job wants his friends to pray with and for him. He needs them to talk *to* God and not talk *for* God.

You can bring such comfort to a friend when you show up and be by their side. You can hold their hand and dry their tears. You can reach out to them and encourage them to confide in you when they are ready. You can help them put their daily life on hold while they deal with great misfortune. It can be a great comfort for them to know you are praying for them.

When a friend is hurting, can you be a helpful spiritual physician and pray with and for them?

Notes:

Job 13:15-18 – Trust in the LORD

*¹⁵"Though He slay me, yet will I trust Him.
Even so, I will defend my own ways before Him.
¹⁶ He also shall be my salvation,
For a hypocrite could not come before Him.
¹⁷ Listen carefully to my speech,
And to my declaration with your ears.
¹⁸ See now, I have prepared my case,
I know that I shall be vindicated."*

Even in his great suffering, Job holds onto his trust in the LORD Almighty. Job believes he has done nothing wrong. Job knows that God can end his suffering by slaying him, but he continues to trust in God's plan.

A hypocrite is someone who presents a false appearance. He is an actor, a pretender. Job knows that a pretender cannot go before the throne of God and win his case. God sees right through our hypocritical pretending and looks straight at our hearts. He knows what we value, what we seek first, and what we hold as most important.

God can see our inward idols, our inflated view of ourselves, and our love for money, power, or social status. We desire to be liked by many and held in high esteem. Yet, we know our own hearts. We know we are very selfish people, caring little for those around us.

Unlike Job, we do not look forward to the time when we will stand before God and He will go over everything we have said and thought about others, and we are forced to admit that our hearts are black, selfish, and wicked.

The only way we can have total trust in God is to know that He is our salvation. We need to remember that we were dead in our sins and we need the Holy Spirit to be born again. We need God to give us a new heart – a heart of flesh instead of our dead heart of stone.

Job knows that he will be vindicated because he trusts in God to be his vindicator.

Can you stop pretending to be wholly righteous and trust the sacrifice of Jesus on the cross to cover your sins?

Notes:

Job 14:1-5 – Our Days Are Numbered

¹ "Man who is born of woman
Is of few days and full of trouble.
² He comes forth like a flower and fades away;
He flees like a shadow and does not continue.
³ And do You open Your eyes on such a one,
And bring me to judgment with Yourself?
⁴ Who can bring a clean thing out of an unclean?
No one!
⁵ Since his days are determined,
The number of his months is with You;
You have appointed his limits, so that he cannot pass."

Job is struggling with incredible suffering and pain. He knows that he came forth like a beautiful flower, loved by his parents, but now he sees himself fading away. His life is fleeing away like a shadow in the bright sunlight. However, he continues to hold onto the Almighty. He knows that his days are numbered by God.

We are such impatient people. No matter what stage of life we are in, we want to rush through that stage and move onto the next. Job is reminding us that our lives will come to an end. This end is not determined by us, but by God Himself.

God has many things to teach Job during this time of suffering. Job needs to know that God is in charge, even in tough times. He needs to learn the value of real friendship so that he can be a great friend when his time of suffering is over. Job needs to learn that he must rely on God in good times and bad times. He needs to learn that God brings blessings, great and small, into our lives each day.

Even on the bad days, there are many things to be grateful for. We are to count our blessings each day, even when we do not feel like a beautiful flower. For, one day, our time here on earth will be over. As Psalm 144:4 says, "Man is like a breath; his days are like a passing shadow." Now is the time to grab hold of our daily blessings. Difficult times will always come to an end.

If you counted your blessings today, would they make an almost endless list?

Notes:

Job 19 – Estranged and Forgotten

*13 "He has removed my brothers far from me,
And my acquaintances are completely estranged from me.
14 My relatives have failed,
And my close friends have forgotten me."
21 "Have pity on me, have pity on me, O you my friends,
For the hand of God has struck me!
22 Why do you persecute me as God does,
And are not satisfied with my flesh?"*

Job uses very strong and despondent language in this section of his lament. His brothers are "removed far" from him, his acquaintances are "completely estranged," his relatives "have failed," and his close friends "have forgotten" him.

These are words of death in our highly-connected world today. We seem to live by our constant connection to other people in our social media universe. In our social lives, we fear being left out, forgotten, or alone, and we strive to be popular. There is not much we won't do to remain popular, connected, liked, and remembered.

In chapter 19, Job feels the pain of being forgotten and left out. He feels estranged from his acquaintances, who are far away and have forgotten him. Job goes on to state that his former friends and acquaintances are persecuting and attacking him. It is bad enough that he feels like the hand of God has struck him; he does not need his friends to pile on to his pain.

We fear being persecuted and attacked. It is one thing to be left out by people and feel the pain of isolation, but being persecuted by others is a whole further level of hurt. Today, people can be so subtle in their attacks, such as making slightly snarky comments or backhanded compliments meant to belittle us. We feel, like Job, that they are digging into our flesh. We, like Job, just want to feel connected, not left out, and loved, not estranged.

Is there someone in your life that might feel estranged or left out? If so, what are you going to do about it?

Notes:

Job 19:25-27 – My Redeemer Lives

*²⁵ "For I know that my Redeemer lives,
And He shall stand at last on the earth;
²⁶ And after my skin is destroyed, this I know,
That in my flesh I shall see God,
²⁷ Whom I shall see for myself,
And my eyes shall behold, and not another.
How my heart yearns within me!"*

Although Job is suffering, he knows that somehow God is still in charge of his life. He just doesn't understand how God can be in charge and yet inflict so much suffering. In the midst of his pain and confusion, Job gives up on trying to figure it all out. He doesn't want to wrestle with himself and God on why everything is going wrong. Job is finally giving up and giving it all to God.

Job tells God he has given up on trying to figure this all out. Instead, he will rely on the fact that God is his Redeemer. Job is going to trust God in the midst of his pain and allow God to walk with him through it.

Job calls God his "Redeemer." To "redeem" means to pay to take possession of something. Job holds onto the fact that God is going to redeem him out of the mess he is in. Even after his body dies, he will see God. Job yearns with all his heart to see God face to face. More than anything, Job wants to be with God, even if he still has to go through a time of suffering.

Job is pointing us toward the Messiah, Jesus. Jesus was perfectly sinless while living on the earth. Jesus is the one who redeemed us by paying for our sins with His death on the cross. Jesus paid the great price so that we might have our sins washed away and our souls made white as snow.

Jesus defeated suffering and death by taking it upon Himself. Your Redeemer lives! If you have repented of your sinful path, if you have given God control, if you have accepted Jesus as your Redeemer, know that you will see Him face to face.

If you have not accepted Jesus as your Redeemer, are you ready to do this now?

Notes:

Job 20:4-8 – Where Is God's Justice?

*⁴ "Do you not know this of old,
Since man was placed on earth,
⁵ That the triumphing of the wicked is short,
And the joy of the hypocrite is but for a moment?
⁶ Though his haughtiness mounts up to the heavens,
And his head reaches to the clouds,
⁷ Yet he will perish forever like his own refuse;
Those who have seen him will say, 'Where is he?'
⁸ He will fly away like a dream, and not be found;
Yes, he will be chased away like a vision of the night."*

In this passage, Job's friend Zophar discusses why God allows the wicked to prosper. We all struggle with why this occurs. Why is my life so messed up, even though I try to be good? Others around me don't even make an effort to be good, and they lie, cheat, and steal to take advantage of others. They seem to be doing fine. Why does God allow this?

Zophar reminds us to look beyond today and the bounty of the wicked. He tells us that time is short for the wicked. The two-faced hypocrite is living a shallow life without any real joy in his heart. He will perish like his own refuse or "dung." This is pretty descriptive language for the Bible!

When we are going through great mental or physical suffering, we often think that we cannot stand it one more minute. When we struggle to make it through that one minute, we see a million more minutes of suffering ahead of us. How can we get through this? We want to reach up to the clouds and grab onto something solid, or hold someone's hand for support.

Zophar is trying to remind us that we can get through this because God is willing to suffer along beside us. God will be with us every step of the way. If we can grab hold of the idea that God is with us, He can bring deep joy to our broken hearts. By grabbing onto God's hand, we can have lasting joy that is not "for a moment." However, the hypocrite will perish like his own refuse. The choice is yours; how do you want to live out your life?

Can you grab onto God's powerful right hand and allow Him to walk with you today?

Notes:

Job 21:13-15 – Why Do We Need God?

*13"They spend their days in wealth,
And in a moment go down to the grave.
14 Yet they say to God, 'Depart from us,
For we do not desire the knowledge of Your ways.
15 Who is the Almighty, that we should serve Him?
And what profit do we have if we pray to Him?'"*

Job's world is very much like our own in that the wicked prosper. They spend their days in wealth. They think they have no need for God. They have no desire to know of His ways. They want to spend their time studying the ways of the world and do not want to serve the Almighty. They want to become the almighty of this world.

So why do we need God if the wicked do so well without him?

Perhaps a better question is why do we need to work so hard to succeed in this world? As we acquire wealth, we ask ourselves, "Is this enough?" It is said that John D. Rockefeller was once asked, "How much money is enough?" He responded, "Just a little bit more."

We all strive for wealth. We think that we do not need the knowledge of God's ways. What profit, financially or in our souls, do we get if we pray to Him?

Job is a godly man and he is struggling with the fact that the wicked prosper. It does not seem fair. At this time in Job's suffering, he forgets that God gave him wealth to be used for the good of others. Job knows that the things wealth brought did not bring him joy and peace. The things of the world were meant to be used to serve others. Job was generous with his time and resources. As we will see later, he "caused the widow's heart to sing for joy" (Job 29:13).

Job knew how to use his wealth, for he knew that the things wealth can buy do not satisfy the heart. As Bill Bright once wrote,

> "There is a God-shaped vacuum in the heart of every man which cannot be filled by any created thing, but only by God the Creator, made known through Jesus Christ."

Woe to those who do not desire to know God's ways and do not want to serve Him. They are doomed to always be searching for peace and fulfillment and never finding it.

Can you ask God to draw near to you and ask Him to show you His ways?

Notes:

Job 22:22, 25-26 – Lay Up His Words in Your Heart

*²² "Receive, please, instruction from His mouth,
And lay up His words in your heart."*

*²⁵ "Yes, the Almighty will be your gold
And your precious silver;
²⁶ For then you will have your delight in the Almighty,
And lift up your face to God."*

In Eliphaz's final discussion with Job, he lays some great pearls of wisdom and insight before Job. Eliphaz encourages Job to take instruction from God and to lay up God's word in his heart. The Almighty and His word will be Job's silver and gold.

We do not want to take instruction from God or lay up His word in our hearts. We would rather take instruction and advice from the world. We get information and instruction from so many news and social media sources. We spend hours each day checking our social media feeds and messages. We fear missing out on conversations and updates, and we check our digital streams constantly.

At the end of the day, in the quiet and solitude of our own minds, we realize that the day's information entertained us, but it did not nurture our souls at all. We still feel empty.

We need to lay up God's word in our hearts. We need to read little snatches of it at time. At other times, we need to sit down and read large sections. When was the last time you read one of Paul's letters as a love letter to your church friends? When was the last time you read the history sections of the Old Testament like adventure stories of real men and women struggling to live their lives alongside God Almighty? When was the last time you read the Psalms as songs and poems of godly men struggling through the deep issues of life, or singing praises to God Almighty? When was the last time you read the wisdom literature, like Proverbs, to learn a wise nugget for your day?

God gives us His word as silver and gold. It is precious and it is to be our delight. For when we lay up His word in our hearts, we will see who God is. We will begin to see the face of God and perhaps we will fall in love with Him all over again.

Is today a good day for you to curl up with God's word and read it just for enjoyment?

Notes:

Job 25:2-3, 26:14 – Love and a Small Whisper of Him

² "Dominion and fear belong to Him;
He makes peace in His high places.
³ Is there any number to His armies?
Upon whom does His light not rise?"
[Bildad]

¹⁴ "Indeed these are the mere edges of His ways,
And how small a whisper we hear of Him!
But the thunder of His power who can understand?"
[Job]

In Bildad's last speech to Job, he gives up on convincing Job of his great sin. Instead, Bildad choses to focus on who God is. Like Job, Bildad does not really know why Job is suffering so much.

When we are going through great trouble, it does us little good to concentrate on asking why God has done this to us. Sometimes there are terrible consequences of our sinful actions. When this is the case, we need to own up to our evil acts and ask for forgiveness. However, there are other times when bad things come our way and we don't know why.

There is little value in focusing on the bad around us. However, as Bildad urges Job, there is great value in focusing on God and His splendor. Dominion, sovereignty, and control belong to Him, and no one can take them away from Him. His armies are great in number – no enemy can defeat them. God is beyond us and He brings peace and light to a dark world.

Job responds with "If we only knew!" We only see the mere edges of God's power, might, wisdom, and mercy. We see just a small whisper of His majesty. When God reaches out to the world with His full power, He completely overpowers us and we cannot understand it. He chooses to love us even though we understand so little of Him.

This is one of the reasons why Jesus came to earth, born to a poor family in a tiny village. God knew that we could not understand Him in all His glory, so He poured His glory into the form of a human baby. Jesus grew up in our midst to perfectly show us what it means to be a godly person, and what it means to know God, His word, and His ways. He also showed us what it means to really love God with all our heart, soul, mind, and strength, and what it means to love our neighbors as ourselves. Jesus did this so that we could perceive a whisper of God Almighty.

Can you take time today to focus on how great God's love really is?

Notes:

Job 28 – Where Can Wisdom Be Found?

*12 "But where can wisdom be found?
And where is the place of understanding?
13 Man does not know its value,
Nor is it found in the land of the living.
14 The deep says, 'It is not in me';
And the sea says, 'It is not with me.'
15 It cannot be purchased for gold,
Nor can silver be weighed for its price."*

*23 "God understands its way,
And He knows its place."*

*28 "And to man He said,
'Behold, the fear of the Lord, that is wisdom,
And to depart from evil is understanding.'"*

Job has heard enough from Eliphaz, Bildad, and Zophar. They and Job have not come any closer to answering the question of why bad things happen in our lives. So Job takes a break from this difficult intellectual question and decides that there is much more value in focusing on wisdom. Where can wisdom be found? Who knows where it lives? How do we get more of it?

Job acknowledges that none of us know the value of wisdom. We love our opinions and we love to get them out into the public space. But in the end, our opinions are just noise. We do not know the value of wisdom, nor do we know where to find it. It is not in the depths of the boundless sea. We cannot buy it. Not only can we not buy it, but we could not afford to buy it if it was for sale.

Only God knows the way to the place of wisdom. Wisdom comes from knowledge and experience blended together with good judgment. We can get knowledge with diligent study of God's word. We can get experience through walking with God on His paths. Good judgment comes from listening to God's voice in our hearts. Job reminds us that this wisdom comes from the fear of the Lord. Fear in this sense means great respect, full submission, and a huge sense of awe. The fear of the Lord comes when we admit that we cannot figure out life on our own. It comes when we admit that we have made a mess of our lives. It comes when we see the splendor of the Almighty and we agree to submit to His lordship.

Can you begin to focus on finding wisdom?

Notes:

Job 29:12-17 – Job's Life of Integrity

¹² "Because I delivered the poor who cried out,
The fatherless and the one who had no helper.
¹³ The blessing of a perishing man came upon me,
And I caused the widow's heart to sing for joy.
¹⁴ I put on righteousness, and it clothed me;
My justice was like a robe and a turban.
¹⁵ I was eyes to the blind,
And I was feet to the lame.
¹⁶ I was a father to the poor,
And I searched out the case that I did not know.
¹⁷ I broke the fangs of the wicked,
And plucked the victim from his teeth."

Job describes some of the good deeds he did in the past. As we read in chapter 1, he lived a life of integrity. He delivered the poor, the fatherless, and the ones who needed help because they had no other helpers.

Job "caused the widow's heart to sing for joy." In his day, widows were at the bottom of the socioeconomic ladder. They were often poor, destitute, and homeless, and were usually depressed and sullen. But Job was generous with his time and resources. He did not just give them a handout – he brought real joy back into their lives.

Not only was Job eyes to the blind and feet to the lame, but he searched out those whom he did not know to better understand how he could help them out.

Job did all this while he was a very busy man. Job was running a large estate. He was also a very important elder in the city and, as such, he was helping to run the city. Because he was wise and walked with God, he was frequently sought out for wise counsel. Although he was busy, Job generously sought out those in need and helped them.

Job is a great model of integrity for our own day. He is a person who delivered the poor, acted as eyes to the blind and feet to the lame, and sought out those in need instead of running away from them. He got to know those in need so that he could best help them. Job knew that they needed more than a meal or a coat; they needed something that would cause their hearts to sing – a friend.

Can you seek out someone in need in your life and cause their heart to sing for joy?

Notes:

Job 30:16-19 – Dust and Ashes

¹⁶ "And now my soul is poured out because of my plight;
The days of affliction take hold of me.
¹⁷ My bones are pierced in me at night,
And my gnawing pains take no rest.
¹⁸ By great force my garment is disfigured;
It binds me about as the collar of my coat.
¹⁹ He has cast me into the mire,
And I have become like dust and ashes."

In Job's final defense, he describes the state of his soul. His soul is poured out. He hurts down to his very bones. He gets no rest from his pain. He feels he has become like dust and ashes.

Dust and ashes are our final days. When we have been totally destroyed and burnt up by life, we feel as though we have no substance left. We are blown away, like dust and ashes in a strong wind. We have totally given up and there is nothing left in us.

If you have ever felt like this, you should take great hope in these verses from the book of Isaiah:

"To proclaim the acceptable year of the LORD,
And the day of vengeance of our God;
To comfort all who mourn,
To console those who mourn in Zion,
To give them beauty for ashes,
The oil of joy for mourning,
The garment of praise for the spirit of heaviness;
That they may be called trees of righteousness,
The planting of the LORD, that He may be glorified."

(Isaiah 61:2-3)

Here Isaiah points forward in time to the coming of the Messiah. The Messiah will bring comfort to all who mourn. He will give them beauty for ashes. Isaiah picks up from where Job is, so totally defeated by life, and proclaims that Jesus can give us beauty for ashes. Even in the worst of times, we can grab onto great hope in the One who is much bigger than we are. He has much more power than us, and He loves us beyond what we deserve.

Can you grab onto Jesus' hand and begin to see that He will make beauty from your ashes?

Notes:

Job 31 – What Is Integrity?

*⁵ "If I have walked with falsehood,
Or if my foot has hastened to deceit,
⁶ Let me be weighed on honest scales,
That God may know my integrity."*

*¹⁶ "If I have kept the poor from their desire,
Or caused the eyes of the widow to fail,
¹⁷ Or eaten my morsel by myself,
So that the fatherless could not eat of it..."*

*¹⁹ "If I have seen anyone perish for lack of clothing,
Or any poor man without covering..."*

*²⁴ "If I have made gold my hope,
Or said to fine gold, 'You are my confidence';
²⁵ If I have rejoiced because my wealth was great..."*

*³² "But no sojourner had to lodge in the street,
For I have opened my doors to the traveler..."*

At the very end of Job's speeches, he describes his life of integrity and details what it means to live a life of integrity. A few selections from his last speech hint at what he means when he talks about a blameless life.

Job was not deceitful. He walked in truth. If his life was weighed on the scales of justice, he would come out in the right. Job helped those less fortunate than himself. He rarely ate alone without sharing his meal with someone who had nothing to eat. He made sure that those in his neighborhood had enough warm clothes to survive cold winter nights.

Job did not put his trust in money and wealth. Job knew that material goods are temporary and are not to be our hope and confidence. He knew that he needed to place his hope in God Almighty.

Job was aware that his life was more than food and the latest clothing style. He knew that integrity comes from seeking first the kingdom of God and His righteousness. If we can seek God first instead of ourselves and our petty problems, we will find God's kingdom. If we can just do that, a life of integrity will follow.

If your life today was placed on the honest scales of integrity, how would you measure up?

Notes:

Job 32-37 – Elihu Talks with Job

A young man named Elihu enters the story late in the game. He wants to tell Job all he knows about life and God. Let's take a look and see what we can learn.

*"Therefore I say, 'Listen to me,
I also will declare my opinion.'"*
(Job 32:10)

We all want to declare our opinions. We always think that we know more about what God is doing than anyone else.

*"For He repays man according to his work,
And makes man to find a reward according to
    his way.
Surely God will never do wickedly,
Nor will the Almighty pervert justice."*
(Job 34:11-12)

Elihu insists that if bad things come into our lives, it must be because we deserve it. Fortunately, this is not true. Sometimes God allows bad things to happen to us so we can grow. Elihu is correct in saying that God will "never do wickedly." When God brings us misfortune, He will never do it out of ill will.

*"Behold, God is mighty, but despises no one;
He is mighty in strength of understanding.
He does not preserve the life of the wicked,
But gives justice to the oppressed."*
(Job 36:5-6)

Elihu correctly acknowledges that God is mighty in strength and understanding. He is a God of justice, but sometimes we do not understand the timing of God's justice. God has infinite power that is ruled by infinite wisdom.

"Behold, God is great, and we do not know Him;
Nor can the number of His years be discovered."
(Job 36:26)

Elihu states that God is not only great, but He is beyond us. We can never know Him completely; we cannot even know how long He has been around.

"He covers His hands with lightning,
And commands it to strike."
(Job 36:32)

Elihu goes on to describe the greatness of God, as seen in His creation. Do we really understand God through His creation? Can we define what He is like by observing the clouds, thunder, and lightning?

"God thunders marvelously with His voice;
He does great things which we cannot comprehend."
(Job 37:5)

If God stepped into your bedroom tonight, what would you two talk about?

Notes:

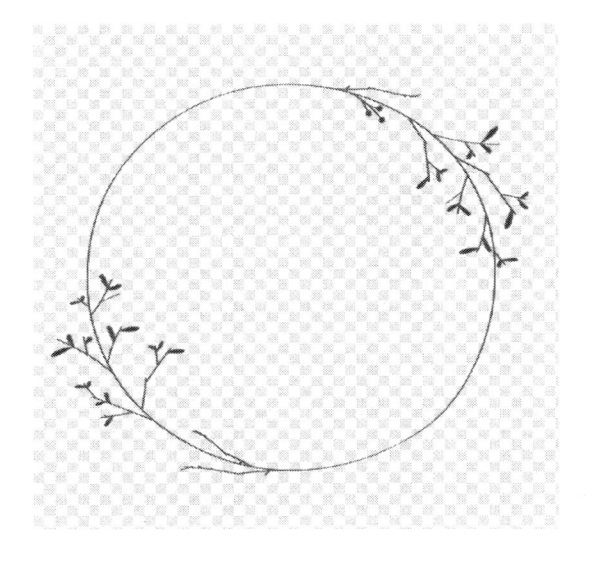

God Shows Up

In the final section of the book of Job, God shows up. He does not spend much time answering Job's questions and objections. Instead, He speaks of His character by describing His creation. You will see many parts of God that we often ignore, much to our detriment. Once you see who God is, you will have a better understanding who you are.

Job 38:1-3 – God Shows Up

¹ Then the L<small>ORD</small> *answered Job out of the whirlwind, and said:*

*² "Who is this who darkens counsel
By words without knowledge?
³ Now prepare yourself like a man;
I will question you, and you shall answer Me."*

Job chapter 38 begins with a bang. God shows up from the midst of a whirlwind, or a violent storm. You may have heard of another occasion where God revealed Himself, this time to the prophet Elijah. In this instance, Elijah was looking for God, but He was not in a great storm, or an earthquake, or a fire; He was in a still small voice. (1 Kings 19:11-12).

Sometimes we think that God only shows up as a still, quiet, small voice in our hearts. Although this is sometimes true, He is not limited to showing up in a small way. Sometimes God shows up in our lives in a big way. This event in Job's life is one of those times, as God chooses to speak to Job out of a violent whirlwind.

God shows up to ask Job who Job thinks he is and who Job thinks God is. God wants to know who darkens His counsel by words without knowledge. He is God Almighty – the omniscient One. Job does not know all sides of the story. He only knows of his personal, human, limited side of the story. He does not know that God is using Job's suffering, and

Job's part in it, to defend His glory and utterly defeat Satan once again.

God is going to help Job see where he stands compared to the Almighty One. God asks Job to prepare himself like one would prepare for a wrestling match. However, in this case, the wrestling match is over wits, knowledge, and character. Before God does anything for Job, He is going to question Job. Job will have to answer God about questions of knowledge, character, strength, and lordship. The purpose of this encounter is for Job to understand more fully who God is and who Job is, for once we understand who God is, then can we understand who we truly are.

If God showed up and challenged you to describe all that He is, what would you say?

Notes:

Job 38:4-6 – The Foundations of the Earth

4 "Where were you when I laid the foundations of the earth?
Tell Me, if you have understanding.
5 Who determined its measurements?
Surely you know!
Or who stretched the line upon it?
6 To what were its foundations fastened?
Or who laid its cornerstone,"

God begins his character wrestling match with Job with a discussion about the foundation of all that is. God wants to know where Job was when He was calling the creation into being. Astronomers believe there are over 1,000,000,000,000,000,000,000,000 solar systems in the universe. If this is true, then there are a lot of suns and planets that make up the universe.

What does the earth stand on? What holds it up? How do we measure everything that holds the earth in its place? Could Job count and measure all the atoms that make up all this?

Foundations have a purpose. Foundations provide stability to a structure, in this case the earth. God wants to know if Job understands the reason why He created the earth and all that is. How do the foundations of creation provide stability? How long will the foundations of the earth provide the earth stability?

God wants to know if Job helped determine the measurements of the earth's foundations. How big is the earth and everything else that holds it all together? If Job were to measure the created universe, where would he stand? What would he use as a measuring stick?

God is trying to get Job to understand the breadth and width of His creation. Not only did God create all that is, but He holds it in His hands. In his letter to the Colossians, Paul states that Jesus creates all things and holds all things together (Colossians 1:16b-17). God did not just create the foundations of the earth and then walk away – He remains intimately involved in His creation by holding it together.

If we could understand even a smidgen of how big the entire creation is, we could begin to understand one aspect of God's character.

If you saw yourself laid out against the scale of all the creation, how would you feel about yourself and the Creator?

Notes:

Job 38:7 – The Stars Sing Together

*⁷ "When the morning stars sang together,
And all the sons of God shouted for joy?"*

God asks Job where he was "when the morning stars sang together." This is an interesting phrase, as we get a small sense of the joy God had in creating all that is. The stars in the sky are not just there to light up our night sky – they too were created to sing in the dance of life together, even though they live in a vast universe. They are filled with the joy of the act of creation itself.

The creation story begins in Genesis 1:3:

"Then God said, 'Let there be light'; and there was light."

How magnificent it would have been to be there when God spoke the creation into being. What did His voice sound like? Was it deep and majestic? Was it loud and overwhelming, or soft and loving, or both at the same time? What language did God use? Probably not English. For that matter, what language does God use in heaven? Again, probably not English. Was there great joy in God's voice when He spoke the creation into being? Did God use one quick word to bring light into the world, or was it a long, drawn-out sound?

Perhaps God did not so much speak the creation into being, but He sang it into being. Imagine God the Father, God the Son, and God the Holy Spirit singing a beautifully complex tercet together as they call all that exists into being. Imagine the bright, powerful notes that called the suns and stars into being, followed by the cooler, solemn tones for the moons and asteroids. Image the majestic glissandos that brought all the trees into being, and the bright dances that brought in the flowers. How would you sing all the animals into being? From the elephants and the lions, to the kangaroos and the koalas? From the foxes and bunnies, to the butterflies and honeybees?

When we sit back and take in the diversity of all God's creation, we begin to get a sense of what it would be like to hear the stars singing together. Try taking some time this week to observe the joyful interplay of all the creation and imagine it singing together.

If you were there when the first morning stars sang together, how would you have felt? How would it have changed you?

Notes:

Job 38:8-11 – Come No Further! Stop!

⁸ "Or who shut in the sea with doors,
When it burst forth and issued from the womb;
⁹ When I made the clouds its garment,
And thick darkness its swaddling band;
¹⁰ When I fixed My limit for it,
And set bars and doors;
¹¹ When I said,
'This far you may come, but no farther,
And here your proud waves must stop!'"

God begins to get more specific about His creation and His power and control over it. He starts by talking about the sea. In general, the Israelites were deathly afraid of the sea. They were people of the land. Job kept sheep, camels, and oxen. He did not like the sudden storms that came up on the Sea of Galilee, and he definitely did not like the Mediterranean Sea. So God grabs Job's attention when He talks about shutting the sea behind strong doors.

God continues to describe the creation of the seas. God states that the sea "burst forth from the womb." This image would have frightened Job. Imagine seeing the waters of the earth bursting forth. Job would have wondered who could stop this rushing water.

God completes this section by describing not just His creative power, but His ruling power. He has set limits on the things that might frighten mankind. He has set bars and doors to hold the waters in their place. When the proud waves crash against the rocks and rise up with their white froth, trying to reach beyond the rocky boundary, God tells them that they must stop!

God gives Job this image to remind him of the power of the physical creation. Water without any boundaries would destroy all that is. But even with all its power, water must still obey the commands of God. Even when a huge storm occurs with high winds and flooding, God still sets boundaries over the water where it can go no further. When God says, "Here your proud waves must stop," they will stop.

We are to take comfort in God's control over the most powerful forces of nature. He still reigns over all of them. He speaks and they obey.

The next time you see a great storm coming, can you take comfort in knowing that God reigns over the storm?

Notes:

Job 38:12-13 – The Dawn Knows Its Place

[12] "Have you commanded the morning since your days began,
And caused the dawn to know its place,
[13] That it might take hold of the ends of the earth,
And the wicked be shaken out of it?"

God discusses a much calmer image – the dawn of a new day. He asks Job if he has ever commanded the morning to start the day.

You may have had the wonderful experience of watching the morning begin. It is fantastic to see the dramatic reds and yellows peek out over the edge of the earth and then see the sun itself rise into the sky. The sky lights up and the hope and joy of a new day begins.

God is going deeper in these verses. He is not just asking Job if he has watched the morning begin, but also if he has commanded the morning to begin the day. Imagine a terrible storm at night. The wind is howling and the rain is beating on your roof. The electricity is out in your home and you have only one small candle lit. The storm rages on and the candle is burning down. Finally, the candle goes out and you are left in total darkness in a raging storm. You cannot wait for the dawn to come. But it seems that for hours and hours there is only darkness and the fierce storm. You wish that you knew the place of the dawn. You wish you had the power to command the dawn from its place so the morning would begin. You know the dawn would have no effect on the raging storm, yet the dawn would bring hope.

This is what God is trying to get Job to see. God is the One who brings hope to a dark world. God is the One who brings hope to a dark soul. Often we cannot manufacture hope in our hearts when we are in the midst of a raging personal storm. God can bring hope from outside our hearts. Just as He commands the dawn to bring the morning, God can bring hope to our lives.

Can you get up very early one day this week to see the dawn bring in a new day? Can you see how this can bring hope into your life?

Notes:

Job 38:17 – The Doors of the Shadow of Death

17 "Have the gates of death been revealed to you?
Or have you seen the doors of the shadow of death?"

God has shown Job that He is the Creator of all that is. He brought the stars together to sing when He made them, He commands the waves to stop, and He begins each new day. Now God reminds Job that He controls death.

God uses two dramatic images here: the gates of death and the doors of the shadow of death. Both images strike fear into our hearts. While some of us do not fear death, we all fear the process of dying. This is what God is getting at here. The gates of death are the edge of death. What will we see when we are at the doors of the shadow of death? Will everyone go to heaven? Is there a real hell? How do I know where I will go? Will I be surprised when I step through the gates of death? These are age-old questions that have plagued mankind since the beginning of time.

This is one of the reasons why Jesus' words about life beyond the shadow of death are so comforting. In one such discussion, Jesus says, "In My Father's house are many mansions; if it were not so, I would have told you. I go to prepare a place for you" (John 14:2).

There is a place on the other side of the gates of death. In fact, there is a wonderful mansion being prepared for us. Jesus himself is preparing this place for us. But how do I know if He is preparing a mansion for me?

The Scriptures tell us over and over again that we cannot earn our way into these heavenly mansions by our good works alone. We think that if our good works outweigh our bad works, God will be pleased with us. Unfortunately, our good works can never be good enough to get us into heaven. The reason for this is that our bad deeds pollute us. It is like having straight A's in school, but then disaster strikes and you get a C in one of your classes. You no longer have straight A's and there is nothing you can do to get back to straight A's. God is the same way. He does not grade on a curve. Because He is perfect, we must be perfect. But how can we be perfect? Taking on the righteousness of Christ and placing our total trust in Him will make us perfect in God's eyes.

When you look through the doors of the shadow of death, what will you see?

Notes:

Job 38:28-30 – Has the Rain a Father?

²⁸ "Has the rain a father?
Or who has begotten the drops of dew?
²⁹ From whose womb comes the ice?
And the frost of heaven, who gives it birth?
³⁰ The waters harden like stone,
And the surface of the deep is frozen."

God continues talking with Job about His creation. He asks Job if he knows the father of the rain and morning dew. Does Job know the mother of the frost and ice? How can we know this father of the rain? We can understand the science behind the water cycle, but can we understand why God birthed the idea of rain? Why did God not make rain a different way? Perhaps the only kind of rain could have been hail or sleet. That surely would have changed the concept of a warm, soft summer rain. Just the existence of rain points to the creative goodness of God.

Jesus brings up rain again in the Sermon on the Mount in Matthew 5:43-45. He is talking to His followers about loving their neighbors – not just the nice neighbors, but the mean neighbors as well. He tells us to love all our neighbors, even to the point of asking God to bless those who curse us. Jesus closes this illustration with the idea of rain. God sends rain to the just as well as the unjust. We call this "God's common grace." God does good things for everyone, even for those who hate Him. Why does He do this? That is a good question. Those who hate God certainly do not deserve His grace.

God does good things for all of us so we can see His mercy, learn of His lovingkindness, and know of His goodness and greatness. He also uses this as an object lesson for His followers, that it might be an example of what it means to love our neighbors.

We get all these lessons just by knowing that God is the Father of rain! Next time you are in a rainstorm, look past the inconvenience of it. Maybe you can see the object lesson – do good to all your neighbors, whether they are nice or not.

If you do this, would they see a bit of God in you?

Notes:

Job 38:31-32 – The Belt of Orion

³¹ "Can you bind the cluster of the Pleiades, Or loose the belt of Orion? ³² Can you bring out Mazzaroth in its season? Or can you guide the Great Bear with its cubs?"

God takes Job outside on a cold, clear, winter night and tells him to look up at the sky. Job recognizes some of his favorite celestial wonders: the Pleiades, Orion, and the Bear. They bring comfort to Job because of their consistency – they are always in their same places in the night sky.

To help Job see who he really is in comparison to God Almighty, God asks Job if he can bind up the seven stars that make up the Pleiades. Can Job loosen the belt of Orion? Job knows that he cannot undo Orion's belt – the stars are millions and millions of miles away. They are so far beyond Job's grasp that he cannot even comprehend their locations in space. The stars that make up Orion were put there by God millions of years before Job was even born. While staring at these nighttime stars, Job begins to understand God's greatness. Job understands that God could undo the stars that make up the constellation of Orion just as easily as Job could undo the sash on his robe.

Job begins to understand the greatness of God alongside the lovingkindness of God. Even in His greatness, He takes the time to address some of Job's concerns. Job is blown away when he begins to grasp that the One who put the constellations in the sky is the same One who listens to his prayers.

God is willing to take care of our every need. He can be the Creator of all that is and at the same time hear and respond to our individual prayers. He can be a loving Father to each of every one of us.

The next time you get a chance to look at the night sky, especially the winter night sky when Orion is present, try to hold these two thoughts in your head:

1. God made these constellations for you and Job. These star patterns are huge – millions of miles apart.
2. God cares about your individual prayers. He wants to hear from you.

Can you hold these two thoughts in your head?

Notes:

Job 38:36 – Understanding to the Heart

³⁶ "Who has put wisdom in the mind?
Or who has given understanding to the heart?"

God continues His discussion with Job with a more personal thrust. Instead of talking about the wind and rain or the stars and lightning, He is talking about the human mind and heart.

He first talks about wisdom in the human mind. Wisdom is the combination of knowledge, experience, and good judgment. There are many places in Scripture where we see humans acting foolishly or being called fools. Usually this is because we cannot put our knowledge and experience together in such a way that we can make good judgments. Left on our own, we seem to have a propensity to make foolish judgments.

God continues to probe deeper, asking, "Who has given understanding to the heart?" At times, the human heart can be dark and wicked. We do not love our neighbors as ourselves, and sometimes we hate them. Moreover, we do not love God – we despise Him. Even when we see all the good common grace He sends our way, we still want nothing to do with Him. We want to act like we are the supreme rulers over our own lives and all that is.

The Scriptures describe the human heart as a heart of stone:

"I will give you a new heart and put a new spirit within you; I will take the heart of stone out of your flesh and give you a heart of flesh." (Ezekiel 36:26)

Even if we come to the point where we see our own hearts of stone, we are powerless to change them. This verse in Ezekiel makes it clear that the reason we cannot change our hearts is that they are as hard as stone. Only God can come into our lives, break our hearts of stone, and change them into living hearts of flesh. Only God can transform our hearts so that we may have a real understanding of who He is and then who we are. We cannot do it ourselves. We need Him to do it.

If you have never asked Jesus to come into your heart of stone and make it a living heart of flesh, can you do that today?

Notes:

Job 39:1-4 – The Wild Mountain Goats

¹ "Do you know the time when the wild mountain goats bear young?
Or can you mark when the deer gives birth?
² Can you number the months that they fulfill?
Or do you know the time when they bear young?
³ They bow down,
They bring forth their young,
They deliver their offspring.
⁴ Their young ones are healthy,
They grow strong with grain;
They depart and do not return to them."

God reminds Job that there is much that goes on in the world that Job is totally unaware of. Here He talks about the mountain goats and the deer. Does mankind with all its science and knowledge know every minute detail about mountain goats? Does Job know everything about how mountain goats survive in their rocky, remote habitats? Does he know exactly when a mother goat is pregnant? Exactly when and where her baby is born? How does she help the young ones begin healthy lives and grow strong and independent?

Job was an important elder of the city. He helped run the city and served as a wise counselor. People came to him for instruction and assistance. As important as we think we are, there is so much going on all around us that we know nothing about.

God, on the other hand, is involved in the lives of the mountain goats and the deer. God cares about the birds of the air and the lilies of the fields. There are many parts of the creation that we know little about, yet God knows everything about.

What is amazing about this is that while God is engaged with all these hidden aspects of the creation, He still cares about each of us individually. He loves to hear the concerns of our hearts, just as parents love to hear the concerns of their children. Jesus tells us to come to Him, all who labor and are heavy laden, and He will give us rest. He has time for all of us. We just need to see that we are being crushed by our own labors and our own emotional baggage. We need someone to come alongside us who is strong enough and has the time so we can hand off these burdens. God is trying to tell Job that not only does He care about each of the solitary mountain goats, also He cares about each of us.

Can you stop trying to carry your own burdens alone and hand them off to Someone who can handle them for you?

Notes:

Job 39:26-28 – Does the Eagle Mount Up?

*²⁶ "Does the hawk fly by your wisdom,
And spread its wings toward the south?
²⁷ Does the eagle mount up at your command,
And make its nest on high?
²⁸ On the rock it dwells and resides,
On the crag of the rock and the stronghold."*

God discusses hawks and eagles to remind us of strength and freedom. He first asks Job if he gives the hawk wisdom to know how to soar and where to fly. Does Job command the eagle to mount on its great wings? Does Job help the eagles find protected places for their nests?

God uses these creatures to remind Job of strength. The hawks and eagles seem to be able to float in the air for hours and hours. From high elevations, they can see their prey on the ground with vision that is much sharper than ours.

Isaiah picked up on this same theme:

"Have you not known?
Have you not heard?
The everlasting God, the LORD,
The Creator of the ends of the earth,
Neither faints nor is weary.
His understanding is unsearchable."
(Isaiah 40:28)

"But those who wait on the LORD
Shall renew their strength;
They shall mount up with wings like eagles,

They shall run and not be weary,
They shall walk and not faint."
(Isaiah 40:31)

Isaiah reminds us of God's strength: "Have you not known? Have you not heard?" How is it that we keep forgetting the LORD is everlasting, unbound by time? As Creator, He is engaged in His creation and He never misses a beat, nor does He grow weary with the task.

Those who wait on the LORD, rest in Him, and give Him their burdens will be renewed by Him. God will renew their lives with new strength and understanding. Those who put their faith and trust in God will mount up with wings like eagles. They will have the strength to run the race of life and finish strong. They will not faint in the time of battle, for God will renew them and uphold them.

Have you forgotten that the LORD is the everlasting God and He does not grow weary?

Notes:

Job 40:9 – Have You an Arm Like God?

*⁹ "Have you an arm like God?
Or can you thunder with a voice like His?"*

God continues to speak to Job out of the whirlwind, telling Job to prepare himself for His questions. He then asks Job if he has an arm like God.

These anthropomorphic statements about God help us to understand something of who He is. Most likely, God does not have eyes and a face or arms like we have. He transcends that in His being. Yet, He still uses these terms to help us understand who He is.

One of God's favorite symbols of His strength is His arm. The arm of God is mighty and strong. Job understands the need for a strong arm, as the arm of a warrior defines his effectiveness in battle.

Isaiah expands on this image:
"Break forth into joy, sing together,
You waste places of Jerusalem!
For the LORD has comforted His people,
He has redeemed Jerusalem.
The LORD has made bare His holy arm
In the eyes of all the nations;
And all the ends of the earth shall see
The salvation of our God."
(Isaiah 52:9-10)

Isaiah describes a time of great joy when the LORD comforted and redeemed His people and made bare His holy arm. When God brings His arm into battle, all the nations, to the ends of the earth, will see the salvation of our God. God is strong enough to bring His will to completion.

Isaiah expands on God's arms and hands:

"Surely, they may forget,
Yet I will not forget you.
See, I have inscribed you on the palms of My hands…"
(Isaiah 49:15b-16a)

God has inscribed our names on the palms of His hands. He is strong and mighty to save us, and He holds us with His lovingkindness. He will not forget those whom He has redeemed. Our names are always before Him, inscribed on His hands.

Can you rest in His arms and His hands?

Notes:

Job 42:1-6 – Job's Response

*¹ Then Job answered the L*ORD *and said:*

*² "I know that You can do everything,
And that no purpose of Yours can be withheld from You.
³ You asked, 'Who is this who hides counsel without knowledge?'
Therefore I have uttered what I did not understand,
Things too wonderful for me, which I did not know.
⁴ Listen, please, and let me speak;
You said, 'I will question you, and you shall answer Me.'*

*⁵ I have heard of You by the hearing of the ear,
But now my eye sees You.
⁶ Therefore I abhor myself,
And repent in dust and ashes."*

Job finally gets a chance to respond to God. Job tells God that He can do anything that He proposes to do. God's creation is too wonderful for Job to completely comprehend. More important, Job has come to understand a bit of who God is. Job has seen God and now he abhors himself. Compared to God, he sees himself with disgust.

There is a battle of wills going on in the world today. Many people are trying to take over, be in charge, and be on top of things. We are always so busy fighting these little skirmishes that we rarely take the time to see that we are not the One in charge. We are not the Supreme Being.

Job got a pretty healthy glimpse of who God is. He got to see God as the Creator of everything and all its diversity. God made the stars and moons, wind and rain, a great menagerie of animals, and you and me. He did all this for His joy and His glory. Job also got a peek into God's mind. He learned that God called all things into creation to be part of an integrated dance. All these different parts of the creation have a role to play in God's great dance of life.

Finally, Job got to see who he is in relation to God and the great dance of life. Yes, God gave Job a role to play in this world (as He does with us today), but not the lead role. Not even close!

Job got to see that he can get the most joy and satisfaction out of life by repenting in dust and ashes. It is only after we ask God for forgiveness for being arrogant in attempting to unseat Him from His throne that we can come into a right relationship with God, ourselves, and the dance of life.

If God were to question you today like He did with Job, what would you say?

Notes:

Job 42:7-8 – Job Shall Pray for You

⁷ And so it was, after the LORD had spoken these words to Job, that the LORD said to Eliphaz the Temanite, "My wrath is aroused against you and your two friends, for you have not spoken of Me what is right, as My servant Job has. ⁸ Now therefore, take for yourselves seven bulls and seven rams, go to My servant Job, and offer up for yourselves a burnt offering; and My servant Job shall pray for you. For I will accept him, lest I deal with you according to your folly; because you have not spoken of Me what is right, as My servant Job has."

God's long speech with Job ends rather surprisingly. God speaks to Job's comforters and He is not pleased. Eliphaz, Bildad, and Zophar did not speak correctly about God and suffering, as Job did. God tells them to go before Job so that Job can pray for them.

There are several reasons why Job is to pray for his friends, the first being that Job is blameless and upright. He fears God and shuns evil. He is a man of integrity. Throughout all his suffering, he holds onto God and His mercy, and he never curses God.

The second reason is that Job has been through great suffering and has come out the other side. When we are in the midst of suffering, we do not know if or when it will end. Will it be the next day or years from now? For example, when Jonah was in the belly of the great fish, he did not know he would be there for three days – it could have been three weeks. He, like Job, probably thought he would die in the midst of great suffering. However, when we make it to the other side of suffering, we have a valuable new perspective on things.

So it is with Job. Job gets a glimpse of God's majesty. From this perspective, he comes to know more deeply what it means to fear God, or understand His awesomeness. Like when we get a glimpse of God's majesty and it rocks us to our very core, we emerge as a new person.

If you are in the midst of comforting a friend going through great suffering, do not give up on them. Remain by their side through it all. If you are the one in the midst of suffering, do not give up on God. He is working all things for His glory. When the suffering is over, take note of who you are and what you have learned about God. Some of the lessons may surprise you.

Are you ready to have a friend pray for you? Might you ask them to pray for you today?

Notes:

Job 42:16-17 – Full of Days

¹⁶ After this Job lived one hundred and forty years, and saw his children and grandchildren for four generations. ¹⁷ So Job died, old and full of days.

Job's story ends with his life being fully restored. It is sort of a bittersweet ending. Job suffered greatly. He lost his sons and daughters, all his material possessions, and his coveted position in society. His relationships between his wife, friends, and comforters were strained. He was physically ill. He lived through hell on earth.

Nevertheless, throughout all this, Job did not curse God. He held onto God and His faithfulness. He knew that God would be his Redeemer either in this life or the next. God chose to redeem Job's life during his time on earth, allowing him to start his life over again. In his new life, Job ends up having seven sons and three daughters, and receives twice as many physical possessions as before. However, the emphasis at the end of the story is not on his physical possessions but on his life.

The book of Job ends with the ancient Hebrew phrase "full of days." This does not mean just a long life; it means a rich life. We get a sense from this phrase that Job lives life to the fullest after his great suffering. He treasures each new day and enjoys his children and grandchildren for four generations. He knows that he has come through a time of great suffering and he is going to live a grateful life each and every day.

God wants us to live with hearts full of gratitude. We do not know what the future will bring, but we can still be grateful for what we have today and for God's faithfulness. He will never leave or forsake His children.

"Be strong and of good courage, do not fear nor be afraid of them; for the LORD your God, He is the One who goes with you. He will not leave you nor forsake you."
(Deuteronomy 31:6)

How might you change your life today to get on the path toward a life full of days?

Notes:

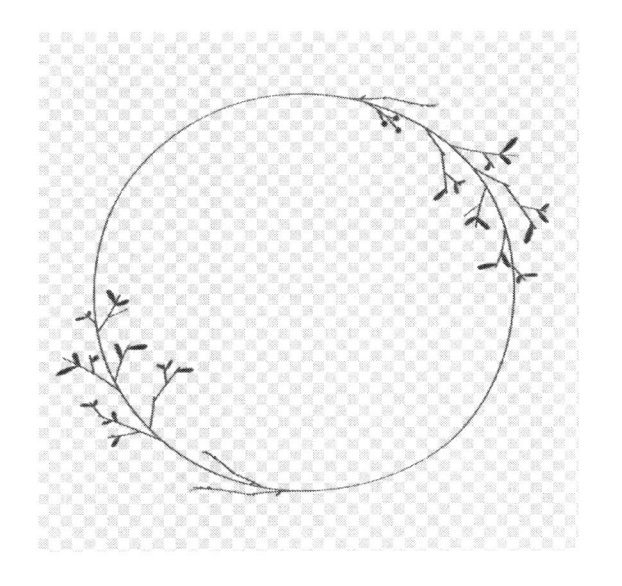

III. The Life of Joseph

In the study of Joseph, you will meet a dysfunctional family, see sibling rivalry, and find Joseph stuck in places that he does not want to be. Finally, you will see God working through Joseph, with the gifts and talents He has given him. At the end of Joseph's story, you will discover that what was "meant for evil, God meant for good."

Genesis 37:2-4 – Joseph's Dysfunctional Family

² This is the history of Jacob.

Joseph, being seventeen years old, was feeding the flock with his brothers. And the lad was with the sons of Bilhah and the sons of Zilpah, his father's wives; and Joseph brought a bad report of them to his father.

³ Now Israel loved Joseph more than all his children, because he was the son of his old age. Also he made him a tunic of many colors. ⁴ But when his brothers saw that their father loved him more than all his brothers, they hated him and could not speak peaceably to him.

Joseph's story starts out when he is just seventeen years old. He is a shepherd with several of his brothers. Being one of the youngest sons of Israel, Joseph often plays the role of a messenger. As a messenger, he is responsible for bringing word from his brothers in the distant pastures to their father, Israel, in town. Joseph is a truthful young man, so when his brothers do something wrong in the pastures, he willingly delivers a bad report about them to Israel. This creates some sibling rivalry between Joseph and his brothers.

To make matters even worse, Israel plays favorites. He is very demonstrative with his love for his son Joseph. He even gives Joseph a very expensive, colorful tunic. Bright dyes for clothing were rare and expensive in Joseph's day because all the dyes were natural, coming from flowers or insects. Joseph flaunts his father's favoritism in front of his brothers by wearing his special tunic, causing them to hate him even more. They cannot even speak peaceably to Joseph.

While Joseph has a special relationship with his father, his relationship with his brothers is horrible. Part of the reason for this sibling rivalry is that Israel's twelve sons came from four mothers. Israel wanted to marry Rachel, but was tricked into marrying her sister, Leah. After Jacob married Rachel, Leah and Rachel got into a contest to see who could produce the most sons for Israel. Then they brought their servants, Zilpah and Bilhah, into the mix as surrogate wives.

Can you imagine Thanksgiving dinner with this family? Four mothers, twelve sons, at least one daughter, all vying for the father's attention. No wonder the brothers hated the special attention Joseph got from their father. Surprisingly, this is the family background of the person God chose to save Israel's family.

If God can use Joseph, who comes from this horribly dysfunctional family, can God use you?

Notes:

Genesis 37:5-8 – Dreams

⁵ Now Joseph had a dream, and he told it to his brothers; and they hated him even more. ⁶ So he said to them, "Please hear this dream which I have dreamed: ⁷ There we were, binding sheaves in the field. Then behold, my sheaf arose and also stood upright; and indeed your sheaves stood all around and bowed down to my sheaf."

⁸ And his brothers said to him, "Shall you indeed reign over us? Or shall you indeed have dominion over us?" So they hated him even more for his dreams and for his words.

Joseph has a dream. It is not his fault that he has this dream – he does not create dreams. God gives him the dream for a purpose. Joseph decides to share his dream with his brothers. When they hear about Joseph's dream, they go ballistic. They say, "Do you think you, the young brother, will reign over us?" It is hard to imagine, but Joseph's family situation gets even worse. His brothers hate him all the more.

Joseph is probably struggling with the idea of sharing his dream with his brothers. He probably thinks it's a really bad idea. However, he shares his dream anyway. This dream has something to do with the future, so it is important that everyone knows about it. Joseph shares his dream and he gets lambasted by his brothers.

This happens to us sometimes. We do what we feel God is telling us to do and we get negative comments from our friends and family. Paul talks about this in his letter to the Ephesians:

"For we are His workmanship, created in Christ Jesus for good works, which God prepared beforehand that we should walk in them." (Ephesians 2:10)

Whenever we get negative comments for doing what we feel God has asked us to do, remember what Paul says. We are God's workmanship, and we are created for good works. Most important, God has prepared the good works beforehand for us. He has done the hard preparation work. All we need to do is walk in the good works.

This is the purpose of Joseph's dream. He gets a glimpse of the good works that God is preparing. Joseph's task is to walk in them. God does not say that the walk will be easy, but the hard preparation work is done. The end is assured.

Do you feel that God is giving you a dream to follow? Are you ready to go walk in the good works which He has prepared beforehand for you?

Notes:

Genesis 37:18-20 – Conspire to Kill Him

¹⁸ Now when they saw him afar off, even before he came near them, they conspired against him to kill him. ¹⁹ Then they said to one another, "Look, this dreamer is coming! ²⁰ Come therefore, let us now kill him and cast him into some pit; and we shall say, 'Some wild beast has devoured him.' We shall see what will become of his dreams!"

Joseph has been sent by his father to go check on his brothers and give them some supplies from home. The brothers are 40 or 50 miles away from home in some distant pasture, tending to the family flocks. Being that far away, it takes weeks to send messages to and from their father. So Joseph goes to find them and to give them good tidings from home.

Joseph's brothers see him far off in his fancy, brightly-colored tunic. They conspire to kill him. They are far from home, so they figure they can get their revenge on him. The depth of their hatred is hard to imagine, but it runs very deep.

Hatred is a very powerful and deep-seated emotion that has wrecked many families. Jesus has some very surprising words on hate:

"You have heard that it was said, 'You shall love your neighbor and hate your enemy.'" But I say to you, love your enemies, bless those who curse you, do good to those who hate you, and pray for those who spitefully use you and persecute you, that you may be sons of your Father in heaven…" (Matthew 5:43-45a)

We know about loving our neighbors. We are good at hating our enemies. Jesus turns this on its head by saying that we are to love our enemies. We are to pray for them, that God will bless them. Jesus ends with "that you may be sons [and daughters] of your Father in heaven."

This is the message from Joseph's life and from Jesus' sermon. We cannot just love the people who are easy to love – we must love the people who are hard to love. While they feel like enemies today, God may work through them in the future.

Is there a Joseph in your life that you need to reach out to in love?

Notes:

Genesis 37:23-28 – Sell Him

23 So it came to pass, when Joseph had come to his brothers, that they stripped Joseph of his tunic, the tunic of many colors that was on him. 24 Then they took him and cast him into a pit. And the pit was empty; there was no water in it.

25 And they sat down to eat a meal. Then they lifted their eyes and looked, and there was a company of Ishmaelites, coming from Gilead with their camels, bearing spices, balm, and myrrh, on their way to carry them down to Egypt. 26 So Judah said to his brothers, "What profit is there if we kill our brother and conceal his blood? 27 Come and let us sell him to the Ishmaelites, and let not our hand be upon him, for he is our brother and our flesh." And his brother listened. 28 Then Midianite traders passed by; so the brothers pulled Joseph up and lifted him out of the pit, and sold him to the Ishmaelites for twenty shekels of silver. And they took Joseph to Egypt.

Joseph's brothers are conspiring to kill him, but they cannot quite agree on how and when. So they throw Joseph into a deep pit used to capture water during the rainy season. After they cast him into the pit, they sit down to lunch. Can you believe this? Joseph is down in the pit, screaming his head off to be rescued by his brothers, and they are sitting around joking and eating lunch. Joseph is calling out to each brother individually, begging and bargaining with them, but to no avail.

Near the end of lunch, they see a caravan of Ishmaelites coming from the north, heading down to Egypt. Judah comes up with the bright idea that instead of killing Joseph, they can sell him to the Ishmaelites. The brothers sell Joseph and make some money on the deal. The brothers do not have guilty consciences because they did not kill Joseph. They dip Joseph's tunic in goat's blood to convince their father that he was eaten by a wild animal. This is one of the greatest shames in the Scriptures, where a set of brothers sell one of their own and then lie to their father about it.

But what about Joseph's dream? What about God's plan for this family? God's plan cannot be thwarted. We see God working through the sinful act of the brothers by having a caravan head to Egypt. A key part of God's plan and Joseph's dream is for Joseph to get to Egypt. Joseph does not expect to be sold to a caravan of traders. At this time, Joseph cannot see God working through his brothers' sinful act. However, Joseph holds onto the dream God gave him and God's promise.

Do you feel like you are on a caravan journey right now? If so, reach out to God and ask for His strength and wisdom.

Notes:

Genesis 37:31-35a – Comfort Him

³¹ So they took Joseph's tunic, killed a kid of the goats, and dipped the tunic in the blood. ³² Then they sent the tunic of many colors, and they brought it to their father and said, "We have found this. Do you know whether it is your son's tunic or not?"

³³ And he recognized it and said, "It is my son's tunic. A wild beast has devoured him. Without doubt Joseph is torn to pieces." ³⁴ Then Jacob tore his clothes, put sackcloth on his waist, and mourned for his son many days. ³⁵ And all his sons and all his daughters arose to comfort him...

Joseph's brothers take his brightly-colored tunic and cover it in goat's blood. They take it to their father and ask, "Do you know whether it is your son's tunic or not?" Of course, he knows it is Joseph's tunic – it is a custom-made, one-of-a-kind tunic. The brothers know it is Joseph's tunic because they took it from him. This is the first level of deception in this story.

Joseph's father, Jacob (also known as Israel), laments that a wild beast has killed Joseph. Jacob goes into a state of mourning for many days. When Jacob declares that a wild beast has devoured Joseph, none of the brothers step forward to denounce the deception. This is the second level of deception, and the depth of deception in this story gets even deeper.

Jacob mourns his favorite son's death for many days and all his sons and daughters try to comfort him. This time is horribly difficult and uncomfortable for Joseph's brothers. Day after day, they lie to their father about what happened to Joseph. They meet with each other and whisper about the deception and whether or not they should tell the truth. Word leaks out to their sisters and they are sworn to silence in the deception. This deception causes a huge dark cloud to sit over Jacob's house for many, many days. It affects much of the daily life in the household, and yet no one steps forward to tell the truth. Each day, they all get deeper and deeper in the darkness of the lie. The brothers somehow think it will get better over time, but it never does. Like most lies, this will come up to bite them in the future.

So it is with us. We build layer upon layer of deception. We hope it will just go away, but it never does. If you have been living with a deception, is now the time to confess it?

Notes:

Genesis 39:1-4 – The LORD Was with Him

¹ Now Joseph had been taken down to Egypt. And Potiphar, an officer of Pharaoh, captain of the guard, an Egyptian, bought him from the Ishmaelites who had taken him down there. ² The LORD was with Joseph, and he was a successful man; and he was in the house of his master the Egyptian. ³ And his master saw that the LORD was with him and that the LORD made all he did to prosper in his hand. ⁴ So Joseph found favor in his sight, and served him. Then he made him overseer of his house, and all that he had he put under his authority.

Joseph is sold to Potiphar, who is captain of the guard of Pharaoh, the king of Egypt. Joseph starts working a lowly position in the fields. However, the LORD was with Joseph and he was successful in all he did for Potiphar. Potiphar recognizes the good work that Joseph is doing. Everything that Joseph works on prospers. Potiphar then promotes Joseph to work inside his home. Joseph eventually becomes the overseer of Potiphar's entire household and property.

This is an incredible story of advancement. It all comes from the fact that the LORD is with Joseph and He makes all his work prosper. Notice that Joseph does not prosper because of his own intelligence, gifts, or talents. When Joseph first showed up at Potiphar's property, what known skills did he have? He worked with sheep in the fields and he delivered messages from his father to his brothers – that was about it. Joseph did not have any great administrative talents or financial talents, and he certainly did not have any great people management skills. God formed all these talents in Joseph so he can one day save the nation of Israel.

Joseph also has a role in these growing talents. He has to work hard to learn these new tasks. He has to work hard to learn the Egyptian language and culture. God uses Joseph's work at Potiphar's property as a proving ground. It is a step along the way and not the end game.

Similar to Joseph, God is currently growing our own talents. This season in our lives is just a stepping stone. It is not the endgame. Can you ask God to show you what gifts and talents He is growing in you right now?

Notes:

Genesis 39:6b-9 – Lie with Me

⁶ᵇ Now Joseph was handsome in form and appearance.

⁷ And it came to pass after these things that his master's wife cast longing eyes on Joseph, and she said, "Lie with me."

⁸ But he refused and said to his master's wife, "Look, my master does not know what is with me in the house, and he has committed all that he has to my hand. ⁹ There is no one greater in this house than I, nor has he kept back anything from me but you, because you are his wife. How then can I do this great wickedness, and sin against God?"

All is going well with Joseph's life. He has a great job managing all of Potiphar's affairs, but he is lonely. He is in a distant land. He is learning to master the Egyptian language. He is learning new customs, new food, and new music. As difficult as life was with his brothers, he misses them. He misses his sisters and most of all he misses his father.

This part of the story takes a twist with "Joseph was handsome in form and appearance." This is a sentence of great forboding. Potiphar's wife notices how handsome Joseph is and how lonely he is. She "cast longing eyes on Joseph." As Potiphar's wife, she commands him to "lie with me." But Joseph refuses. It would be so easy to give in to the temptation. It would feel so good. Who would know? Who would be hurt by this?

Joseph does not give into the temptation for two reasons. First, he cannot do this great wickedness against Potiphar. Potiphar gave Joseph this great position of managing the entire household. He could still be in the fields doing hot, back-breaking work. No, he cannot do this against Potiphar.

More importantly, Joseph cannot do this as a sin against God. Joseph has not forgotten about God and the dreams He gave him. Even though Joseph is distantly separated from his family, his homeland, and his religion, he holds onto God and His promises. Joseph knows that God will not forsake him and therefore he cannot sin against God. Joseph refuses to give into the temptation.

Temptation is so hard to resist. Can you ask God to help you resist temptation today?

Notes:

Genesis 39:20-23 – The LORD Was with Him Again

²⁰ Then Joseph's master took him and put him into the prison, a place where the king's prisoners were confined. And he was there in the prison. ²¹ But the LORD was with Joseph and showed him mercy, and He gave him favor in the sight of the keeper of the prison. ²² And the keeper of the prison committed to Joseph's hand all the prisoners who were in the prison; whatever they did there, it was his doing. ²³ The keeper of the prison did not look into anything that was under Joseph's authority, because the LORD was with him; and whatever he did, the LORD made it prosper.

Joseph had been accused of attempting to rape Potiphar's wife. Even though Joseph had only been faithful to Potiphar, and Potiphar knows this, he has no choice but to side with his wife. She is his wife while Joseph is a foreigner, an outcast, a worker, and worst of all, a Hebrew, not an Egyptian.

So Potiphar has Joseph thrown into prison. Because Potiphar is captain of the king's (or pharaoh's) guard, Joseph is thrown into the prison for the king's prisoners. God is working through these circumstances on several levels. The first is that this is a slightly "better" prison, as it is the king's prison. At least Joseph is fed while in this prison. The second level is that Joseph will need to have a connection to the pharaoh several years from now.

However, Joseph cannot see how God is using this for good in his life. He is probably angry at God, confused by the circumstances. He is feeling sorry for himself and once again feeling totally dejected. Joseph is probably thinking, "What did I do to deserve this?"

Somehow Joseph hangs on to his faith in God. He holds on to the dreams God gave him and decides to make the best of a very bad situation. The LORD is with Joseph and shows him mercy. This allows Joseph's work to earn him favor in the sight of the prison keeper. We can assume that the prison keeper is not a person who is easily impressed. Yet, Joseph impresses him with his hard work and his great administrative skills. Soon Joseph is running a prison filled with very tough and ruthless characters. Joseph is able to do this because the LORD is with him.

Again, it is not Joseph's intelligence and good looks that make him prosper. It is that Joseph does not lose his faith in God. The LORD makes Joseph's work prosper. But remember, Joseph still did the work.

If you feel like you are in prison, ask the LORD what He would have you do while you are there. How does the LORD want to make you prosper?

Notes:

Genesis 40:23-41:1 – Did Not Remember Joseph

²³ Yet the chief butler did not remember Joseph, but forgot him.

¹ Then it came to pass, at the end of two full years, that Pharaoh had a dream; and behold, he stood by the river.

Joseph is still in the pharaoh's prison. The LORD has enabled him to manage the prison for the prison keeper. "The keeper did not look into anything that was under Joseph's authority, because the LORD was with him…" (Genesis 39:23). This was the best-run prison in all of Egypt.

Several years later, Joseph gets two new prisoners placed under his care. One is Pharaoh's chief baker and the other is Pharaoh's chief butler. After these two are in prison for a while, they each have a vivid and disturbing dream. Joseph notices that they look depressed the next day. This is a sorrow that goes beyond just being thrown out of Pharaoh's most intimate court to being in a stinking prison. They each have a dream that they cannot understand.

Joseph tells them that some dreams come from God and that the interpretation belongs to God. Joseph asks them to tell him their dreams and God will give him the interpretation. The chief butler describes his dream:

"Behold, in my dream a vine was before me, and in the vine were three branches; it was as though it

budded, its blossoms shot forth, and its clusters brought forth ripe grapes. Then Pharaoh's cup was in my hand; and I took the grapes and pressed them into Pharaoh's cup, and placed the cup in Pharaoh's hand."
(Genesis 40:9b-11)

Joseph explains that the three branches represent three days. The chief butler gets a good interpretation of his dream; in three days he will be restored as the chief butler. Sure enough, he is restored as the chief butler in three days. The chief butler is so excited to be back in Pharaoh's court that he forgets about Joseph.

For two long years, Joseph listens for the prison keeper's steps coming to release him. Each day he listens, but no one comes to rescue him. Each night he goes to sleep feeling dejected and forgotten. Each day he struggles to hold onto his faith in God and the dreams He gave him. Each day he is disappointed. This goes on for two full years – 730 entire days – yet Joseph does not give up his faith and hope.

Do you feel like you have been in prison for a long time? Can you hold onto your faith and hope in God for one more day?

Notes:

Genesis 41:14-16 – It Is Not in Me

[14]{.sup} Then Pharaoh sent and called Joseph, and they brought him quickly out of the dungeon; and he shaved, changed his clothing, and came to Pharaoh. [15]{.sup} And Pharaoh said to Joseph, "I have had a dream, and there is no one who can interpret it. But I have heard it said of you that you can understand a dream, to interpret it."

[16]{.sup} So Joseph answered Pharaoh, saying, "It is not in me; God will give Pharaoh an answer of peace."

After two long years of Joseph being forgotten in prison, Pharaoh has two disturbing dreams. He is very troubled by these dreams. He feels that they have an important messaged embedded in them, but he does not know what the message is. Like any good king, he calls his advisers, wise men, and magicians so they can give him the interpretation. However, none of them can interpret the dreams.

Finally, the chief butler remembers Joseph, who interpreted his dream correctly and accurately. Pharaoh calls for Joseph, who is quickly brought up out of the prison. But there is a big problem – Joseph is a mess. He stinks, his clothes are nothing but rags, his hair is a wreck, and his complexion is pallid. He cannot possibly go before Pharaoh like this. The members of Pharaoh's court frantically work on Joseph. While they are cleaning him up, they go over the intricate details of court protocol. Joseph gets instructed on how to stand, when to bow, where to look, when to speak, and how to speak. Joseph is quite bewildered by all of the courtly instructions. Joseph decides that he will hold onto God. God has been with him through all these years. He has not left Joseph, even though times have been tough.

Joseph is brought before the great and mighty Pharaoh. Pharaoh tells Joseph that he has heard he can interpret dreams. The court attendants have been holding their collective breath. So far, so good. This foolish Hebrew prisoner has not made a mistake yet. Then Joseph opens his mouth for the first time to answer Pharaoh and effectively says, "No, Pharaoh – you are wrong." What is Joseph doing? No one says "no" to Pharaoh. Joseph continues and says, "It is not in me. God will give Pharaoh an answer of peace."

When everything is on the line, Joseph humbly takes none of the credit. He gives it to God. When you are in this kind of position before the "kings of your life," will you say "no" and give God all the glory?

Notes:

Genesis 41:37-41 – All People Will Be Ruled by Your Word

³⁷ So the advice was good in the eyes of Pharaoh and in the eyes of all his servants. ³⁸ And Pharaoh said to his servants, "Can we find such a one as this, a man in whom is the Spirit of God?"

³⁹ Then Pharaoh said to Joseph, "Inasmuch as God has shown you all this, there is no one as discerning and wise as you. ⁴⁰ You shall be over my house, and all my people shall be ruled according to your word; only in regard to the throne will I be greater than you." ⁴¹ And Pharaoh said to Joseph, "See, I have set you over all the land of Egypt."

Pharaoh has had two disturbing dreams. He knows that there is an important message in these dreams, but he does not know what the message is. None of his court advisors can interpret the dreams. But Joseph is brought up from prison and, through Joseph, God gives Pharaoh the interpretation of his dreams.

The seven objects in each of the dream scenes represent seven years. God is telling Pharaoh that there will be seven years of great abundance, followed by seven years of famine. Joseph goes on to explain more about God's plan of salvation for Egypt, stating that Pharaoh needs to collect one-fifth of the product during the years of abundance and store it up for the seven years of famine. Joseph tells Pharaoh that he should "select a discerning and wise man, and set him over the land of Egypt" (Genesis 41:33).

Pharaoh sees the wisdom in God's plan as expressed by Joseph. He sees that Joseph is discerning and wise. Pharaoh gives Joseph rule over his house and all his people. This is quite a switch for Joseph. He is in prison one day and the next day he is ruling over all of Egypt.

Joseph cannot believe his good fortune. After so many years in prison, he now has a soft bed to sleep in, as much food as he wants, clean clothes to wear, and a clean bath. He feels like he is in heaven on earth. He has so much power, so many servants, and so many people who must bend to his will.

Then it happens. Joseph sees Potiphar and his wife walking down the street. Joseph is to rule over all people, including these two. They are the ones who threw him into prison. Perhaps Joseph briefly plots his revenge on them, but he chooses to just ignore them. Joseph sees that God is the One who is working behind the scenes. Potiphar and his wife are just instruments that God used to get Joseph in front of Pharaoh.

Joseph has a great opportunity to get revenge on Potiphar and his wife and yet he does not. Would you have resisted the opportunity to get revenge?

Notes:

Genesis 41:46-48 – Joseph Went Throughout the Land

⁴⁶ Joseph was thirty years old when he stood before Pharaoh king of Egypt. And Joseph went out from the presence of Pharaoh, and went throughout all the land of Egypt. ⁴⁷ Now in the seven plentiful years the ground brought forth abundantly. ⁴⁸ So he gathered up all the food of the seven years which were in the land of Egypt, and laid up the food in the cities; he laid up in every city the food of the fields which surrounded them.

Joseph was seventeen when he was sold by his brothers. Thirteen years later, God finally has Joseph ready to do the work that He planned for him. However, this task has nothing to do with the dreams that God gave Joseph. The dreams had Joseph's brothers and parents bowing down to him, but they are not even in the same country as Joseph. Did God get it all wrong?

Joseph wisely continues to trust God and His plan. If it took thirteen years to get out of prison, perhaps it will take longer to reunite with his family. Joseph's task at hand is to be in the service of Pharaoh, so he gets down to work.

Joseph has laid out a plan to gather one-fifth of all the grain during the seven years of abundance. Joseph could have chosen to remain in the palace and just direct his division heads to get the work done. After all, isn't delegation a good management style?

In this case, Joseph knows he cannot delegate the tasks. No one has ever tried to store up this much grain in so many different places for such a long period of time. Joseph knows that transporting the grain would be a huge logistical problem, so he has the grain stored in each city. But in order to store the grain, Joseph first needs to build storehouses big enough to hold all the sands of the sea. Since they need to store the grain for seven years, these storehouses need to keep the grain dry and the rodents out. There are lots of details to be worked out and Joseph jumps right into the task with his whole heart. He is going to make sure that every city and community throughout Egypt is taken care of. This is not someone who is whining about the past – this is someone who is doing whatever task God brings before him.

You may feel that you have been languishing in your particular prison for years and God has finally gotten you out. Are you ready to go throughout the land and do the task that God has given you to do?

Notes:

Genesis 41:53-54, 42:1-4 – Lest Some Calamity Befall Him

53 Then the seven years of plenty which were in the land of Egypt ended, 54 and the seven years of famine began to come, as Joseph had said. The famine was in all lands, but in all the land of Egypt there was bread.

1 When Jacob saw that there was grain in Egypt, Jacob said to his sons, "Why do you look at one another?" 2 And he said, "Indeed I have heard that there is grain in Egypt; go down to that place and buy for us there, that we may live and not die."

3 So Joseph's ten brothers went down to buy grain in Egypt. 4 But Jacob did not send Joseph's brother Benjamin with his brothers, for he said, "Lest some calamity befall him."

Just as God predicted through Joseph, the famine has come. There is famine throughout all the lands, but the Egyptians have the grain that Joseph stored up for them to eat. Israel's family in the land of Canaan do not have enough food. Therefore, Israel (Jacob) sends his sons to Egypt to buy food.

Notice how Israel manages this mission to get food. He does not send just one son, Rueben the oldest, nor does he send all eleven of his sons. He sends his ten oldest sons, but he does not let his youngest son, Benjamin, go on this mission. It has been over twenty years since the brothers sold Joseph. Now Benjamin is a grown man, perhaps in his thirties. However, Israel is still treating him like the baby of the family. Israel tells his other sons he is worried that some calamity may befall Benjamin.

Imagine what the other sons are thinking during their five-day journey to Egypt. "Dad is worried about some calamity befalling Benjamin. What about me? Does Dad even care about me? Why is Dad always looking out for the young ones?"

You can imagine the bickering amongst the brothers during this journey. It probably brings back all those memories of Joseph and his special tunic.

It is hard to picture this family becoming a loving, cohesive family unit. Can you picture your dysfunctional, idiosyncratic family coming together and stopping its bickering? What should you do to help this healing process?

Notes:

Genesis 42:14-17 – Three Days

¹⁴ But Joseph said to them, "It is as I spoke to you, saying, 'You are spies!' ¹⁵ In this manner you shall be tested: By the life of Pharaoh, you shall not leave this place unless your youngest brother comes here. ¹⁶ Send one of you, and let him bring your brother; and you shall be kept in prison, that your words may be tested to see whether there is any truth in you; or else, by the life of Pharaoh, surely you are spies!" ¹⁷ So he put them all together in prison three days.

Joseph's brothers make it to Egypt in one piece. No calamity befell them, nor did they berate each other. Joseph, who is Egypt's food administrator, recognizes them immediately, even though he hasn't seen them in over twenty years. He does not know where his brothers are on the road to true repentance, so he does not reveal who he is to them. It is no surprise that they do not recognize Joseph. He dresses as an Egyptian ruler, he is speaking Egyptian through an interpreter, and of course they think that Joseph is dead.

Joseph wants to see Benjamin among them, but he is not sure of the best way to get Benjamin to come to Egypt. He decides to throw all his brothers in prison for the time being. This is most likely the same prison that Joseph spent many years in. It is the same prison where he waited two years for the chief butler to remember him. He does not tell the brothers how long they will be in prison; he just puts them in as suspected spies.

Imagine the dialogue between the brothers now:

"I told you this was a bad plan."

"I knew I should have stayed back with Benjamin."

"How long are we going to stay in this dark, cold prison?"

Their three-day stay in prison is a foreshadowing of both Jonah and Jesus. Jonah spent three days in the belly of the great fish as a time of reflection that led to his repentance. Jesus spent three days forsaken by God the Father because He bore all our sins –past, present, and future. Jesus broke out of His prison of death to redeem us. Jonah was vomited out of the fish so he could start on his path of repentance.

Do you need some quiet time locked in a "prison" to fully comprehend your path of repentance?

Notes:

Genesis 43:8-9 – I Myself Will Be a Surety for Him

⁸ Then Judah said to Israel his father, "Send the lad with me, and we will arise and go, that we may live and not die, both we and you and also our little ones. ⁹ I myself will be surety for him; from my hand you shall require him. If I do not bring him back to you and set him before you, then let me bear the blame forever."

The brothers have returned to their father, Israel, in the land of Canaan. They have now eaten all the food they bought in Egypt and they are contemplating their next move. The obvious next step is to go back to Egypt to buy more food. Unfortunately, the food administrator (Joseph) says that they must bring their youngest brother, Benjamin. Israel is very distraught over the idea of Benjamin going with them, but he sees little choice. He is not sure how to keep Benjamin safe.

Judah steps up and says that he will be Benjamin's surety. If something happens to Benjamin, Judah will take the blame and make it right.

This is the first time one of the brothers has stepped up to do the right thing. Judah is stepping up to be a surety, or a guarantee. "Surety" is such a great word. It gets across the idea of being completely sure of something, or else there will be a penalty.

Judah is a foreshadowing of what Jesus did for us. When we trust Jesus with our lives and invite Him into our hearts, He guarantees eternal life. Eternal life is forever! He guarantees it. No one can take it away. In John's gospel, Jesus uses a metaphor that Joseph's family would have understood; Jesus describes His children as His sheep:

"My sheep hear My voice, and I know them, and they follow Me. And I give them eternal life, and they shall never perish; neither shall anyone snatch them out of My hand."
(John 10:27-28)

Jesus makes it clear that no one will snatch His children out of His hand. Judah is a foreshadowing of Jesus being a surety for us. Judah is stepping up as a surety for Benjamin. Israel can rest assured with Judah's surety because it means that no one will snatch Benjamin away.

Is there someone in your life that you need to come alongside and be a surety for them?

Notes:

Genesis 43:32-34 – Merry with Him

³² So they set him a place by himself, and them by themselves, and the Egyptians who ate with him by themselves; because the Egyptians could not eat food with the Hebrews, for that is an abomination to the Egyptians. ³³ And they sat before him, the firstborn according to his birthright and the youngest according to his youth; and the men looked in astonishment at one another. ³⁴ Then he took servings to them from before him, but Benjamin's serving was five times as much as any of theirs. So they drank and were merry with him.

Joseph's brothers have returned to Egypt to buy food. Benjamin is with them. It has been more than twenty years since Joseph has seen his best friend and brother, Benjamin. To celebrate, Joseph invites all his brothers to a meal at his home. Joseph is still dressed as a royal Egyptian administrator and he only speaks Egyptian around his brothers. Therefore, he remains separate from his brothers at the meal.

The brothers are really nervous about the invitation to this meal. They have already been thrown into prison once. They are not sure if this is an invitation to a meal or if it is an invitation to an execution.

This has been a very stressful period of time for the brothers. They had to convince their father to let Benjamin come to Egypt with them. During the trip, they worry that some evil will befall them. When they get to Egypt, they are not sure what will happen to them. The head administrator invites them into his personal home. They don't know what is going to happen during the meal. There are all kinds of Egyptian customs that they do not know or understand, and nobody is speaking Hebrew with them.

When they sit down to the meal, they are placed in birth order. How did the Egyptians know their birth order? In addition, there is a grim famine in the land, but despite this, they sit down to a great feast with wonderful food, and Benjamin gets five times as much as everyone else. Joseph's brothers finally get a chance to stop fighting. They get to sit back and enjoy life for once. They decide to eat, drink, and be merry with Joseph.

Much of life is filled with unresolved moments. Sometimes that is okay. It is enough to just enjoy the moment. Can you just enjoy the moment today?

Notes:

Genesis 45:1-4 – Make Everyone Go Out

¹ Then Joseph could not restrain himself before all those who stood by him, and he cried out, "Make everyone go out from me!" So no one stood with him while Joseph made himself known to his brothers. ² And he wept aloud, and the Egyptians and the house of Pharaoh heard it.

³ Then Joseph said to his brothers, "I am Joseph; does my father still live?" But his brothers could not answer him, for they were dismayed in his presence. ⁴ And Joseph said to his brothers, "Please come near to me." So they came near. Then he said: "I am Joseph your brother, whom you sold into Egypt."

Joseph cannot control himself any longer. He knows that these are his brothers standing before him, but they do not know that he is Joseph, their long-lost brother. He looks just like an Egyptian official and he is only speaking Egyptian. Joseph knows it is time for the big reveal, but what will happen if all of Egypt finds out what his brothers had done to him?

Joseph is the great hero of Egypt. He is the one who came up with the plan to save one-fifth of the grain during the seven years of abundance. He is the one who went throughout Egypt overseeing the plan. He is the one who made sure the storehouses were built to his specifications. During these past years of famine, every boy, girl, and family member knew it was Joseph who help put their food on the table. Everyone aspired to have an all-encompassing mind and great administrative skills like Joseph. He is the savior of all Egypt.

If the Egyptians knew that his brothers sold him off to an Ishmaelite caravan, there would be a riot in the city. Every Egyptian would want to string up the brothers. Therefore, Joseph sends everyone out of the room. Once everyone is out of the room, he reveals himself to his brothers. He puts them on the path of total repentance by saying that they sold him into Egyptian slavery so that Egypt might be saved.

Joseph does this big reveal to his brothers in a way that does not make their great sin public. If we want to tell someone of some great transgression that they committed against us, we should do it in private. We do not need to proclaim their transgression to everyone else. It is only to be discussed with those who were involved. Joseph understood this.

If someone has done you great harm and it is time for the big reveal, can you do it in such a way as to protect them and their reputation?

Notes:

Genesis 45:9-11 – Say to Him

⁹ *"Hurry and go up to my father, and say to him, 'Thus says your son Joseph: "God has made me lord of all Egypt; come down to me, do not tarry. ¹⁰ You shall dwell in the land of Goshen, and you shall be near to me, you and your children, your children's children, your flocks and your herds, and all that you have. ¹¹ There I will provide for you, lest you and your household, and all that you have, come to poverty; for there are still five years of famine."'"*

Joseph reveals himself to his brothers. They feel shocked, overjoyed, and guilty all at the same time. They can hardly believe it is really Joseph. They also realize with great despair that they are going to have to tell their father something. They have been lying to him for over twenty years.

Imagine Israel bringing up memories of Joseph every year on Joseph's birthday. He was his favorite son. If only he had not sent him on the journey to give word to his brothers those many years ago. He feels it is all his fault for not being a better father. If only, if only, if only...

The brothers, on the other hand, have encouraged the story of Joseph being devoured by a wild animal. Their father saw the bloody tunic. However, the brothers know they put goat's blood on the tunic. It was not Joseph's blood. What are they going to tell their father when they return?

Joseph steps in to save his brothers. He tells them to hurry and tell their father the good news. Not only is Joseph alive, but God has been working behind the scenes to make Joseph the lord of all Egypt. Joseph is the one who was saving up grain during the years of abundance. Not only that, but the land of Goshen is perfect for grazing their flocks. If the brothers come and bring all their children and grandchildren, they can live together again.

Joseph is telling his brothers that a big part of total forgiveness is forgiving sins committed in the past. God is so good; He can even bring good through our wicked deeds. Joseph gives his brothers words to say to their father that will focus on God and His goodness and the work He has been doing.

Can you see past your daily grievances, big or small, and focus on the good that God is doing?

Notes:

Genesis 45:16-18, 47:5-6 – The Best

¹⁶ Now the report of it was heard in Pharaoh's house, saying, "Joseph's brothers have come." So it pleased Pharaoh and his servants well. ¹⁷ And Pharaoh said to Joseph, "Say to your brothers, 'Do this: Load your animals and depart; go to the land of Canaan. ¹⁸ Bring your father and your households and come to me; I will give you the best of the land of Egypt, and you will eat the fat of the land.

⁵ Then Pharaoh spoke to Joseph, saying, "Your father and your brothers have come to you. ⁶ The land of Egypt is before you. Have your father and brothers dwell in the best of the land; let them dwell in the land of Goshen. And if you know any competent men among them, then make them chief herdsmen over my livestock."

When Pharaoh hears about Joseph's brothers being in Egypt and his father in the land of Canaan, he tells Joseph to have them all come to Egypt and he will give them the best land in Egypt. Part of this is for Pharaoh to express his thanks to Joseph for saving Egypt.

When Israel and all his children and grandchildren show up in Egypt, Pharaoh is pleased. He speaks with some of Joseph's brothers and comes to learn that they are shepherds. The land of Goshen is perfect pastureland for their flocks.

Pharaoh goes on to say that as the Israelites are such good shepherds, they should become the chief herdsmen for all of Egypt. This is quite a shift. Pharaoh is acknowledging that a foreign God, the God of Israel and Joseph, is mighty in power and wisdom. He is acknowledging this because when Joseph first came to him, Joseph could not interpret his dreams, but his God could. His God gave him the plan for saving Egypt. Pharoah has been living with the God of Joseph's plan for the past ten years.

God is still at work in the world, sometimes in big ways and sometimes in small ways. Much of the time He is working through His people, like He did with Joseph. When this happens, people who do not know God will take notice.

This may be happening with you. God may be giving you the best land. God may be placing you in a position for your God-given gifts and talents to shine. If so, can you look past the bad that happened to you and focus on how you might serve God in a mighty way?

Notes:

Genesis 50:19-20 – God Meant It for Good

¹⁹ Joseph said to them, "Do not be afraid, for am I in the place of God? ²⁰ But as for you, you meant evil against me; but God meant it for good, in order to bring it about as it is this day, to save many people alive."

Joseph's story ends with him totally forgiving his brothers. They are afraid that Joseph will punish them for their past sins and betrayal, but he proclaims, "Am I in the place of God?" He closes this discussion with the classic line "but God meant it for good."

This is what we have seen in the lives of Jonah, Job, and Joseph. The world and the Evil One keep throwing setbacks and heartbreak in the way of all three of these men. But in all things, they hold onto God and His faithfulness.

Jonah tries to run away from God, but after spending three days in the belly of a great fish, he gets on the path that God has laid out for him. God does His great work before Jonah arrives at Nineveh by working in the hearts of the Ninevites. Jonah just proclaims the message that God has given him and then he gets to see the results.

Job is a man of integrity and he gets tested by Satan, beyond what any of us could stand. He comes through it all because he knows God has a hedge of protection around him. God is his Redeemer. At the end, Job gets a glimpse of God's majesty, power, creativity, and glory as seen through the creation.

Joseph gets betrayed by his own brothers. He is sold to an Egyptian nobleman and is then thrown in prison, despite being innocent. Joseph remains faithful to God, and God remains with Joseph. He gives Joseph great administrative skills and talents so he can save not only the Egyptian people, but also his own family in the land of Canaan.

Joseph summarizes this study for us with the proclamation that others "meant evil." Real harm is dealt out to all three men: Jonah, Job, and Joseph. They suffer greatly, but they remain faithful to God. They somehow know that while others meant evil against them, God meant it for good. This in no way minimizes the suffering they went through, but it points to the majesty of God, His power, and His wisdom. Even though the world and Satan bring bad things, God works through this for His and everyone else's good.

This is the God that Jonah, Job, and Joseph worshipped. As you go through tough times, can you hold on to the idea that "God means it for good?"

Notes:

Wrap-up – Jonah, Job, and Joseph: Men of Action

Often during times of suffering, we collapse into our own mental fog and we do nothing. This was not so with Jonah, Job, and Joseph.

Jonah endured mental, emotional, and spiritual trauma because God asked him to do something that he did not want to do. He hated the Ninevites and he hated the idea of God calling them to repentance. As a man of action, Jonah tried to run away from God. God captured him, in the belly of a great fish, to give him time to understand who God is and who Jonah is. Jonah then sprang into action and called the Ninevites to repent.

Satan brought great calamity on Job's life. Job mourned in dust and ashes over his life situation, but he was not inactive. He debated with his friends on suffering, the nature of evil, and the character of God. Job also complained directly to God about his situation. God finally responded to Job by displaying His creative power and majesty. Job's life was eventually restored, but not until he prayed for his friends. Praying for his friends was a key step in the restoration of Job's life.

Joseph was unjustly sold into slavery and then thrown into prison. However, he did not sit and pout about his situation. He began to learn and stretch his wings in new skills, particularity in administration and management. Joseph used his prison time to work on these skills. When Joseph was released and placed over the entire Egyptian food program, he was able to move throughout the land directing people in God's plan of action.

Each man showed his reaction to spiritual and physical suffering. Each man used his faith in God to hold onto Him so he would be ready to act on His plan at the right time.

When suffering comes your way, can you grab onto God to have Him give you the strength to be a person of action?

Notes:

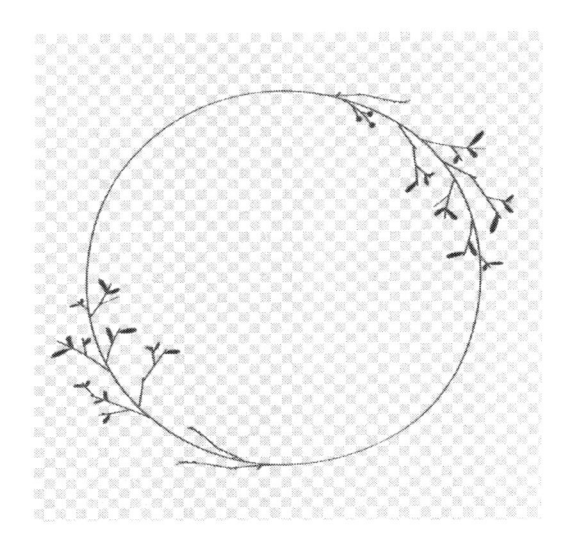

Concluding Thoughts

Hopefully you found some of these devotionals engaging and insightful. This book is meant to be read several times, as some of the Scripture selections will give you a starting point for some internal life-changing moments, depending on what is going on in your life at the time.

This book is based on biblical stories that you might normally read for personal reflection or growth, which is part of this book's power.

Continue to read and continue your spiritual walk, just as Jonah, Job, and Joseph continued their walks with the LORD.

Feel free to reach out at:

tstaylor.devotionals@gmail.com

Acknowledgements

I wish to thank my class at the Church of the Apostles in Atlanta, Georgia. They worked through much of this material, as we learned from the Scriptures together.

Thanks to Will and Tracey Ledbetter for the encouragement and direction to get started.

Thanks to Elayna Ask for the great editing help.

Soli Deo gloria

Made in the USA
Columbia, SC
16 September 2021